HOW A MAN

HANDLES CONFLICT AT WORK

LifeSkills for Men

Also of Interest

9610

LIFESKILLS
FOR MEN

HOW A MAN

HANDLES CONFLICT AT WORK

PAUL TOMLINSON

DAVID HAZARD, *General Editor*

BETHANY HOUSE PUBLISHERS
MINNEAPOLIS, MINNESOTA 55438

Published by Bethany House Publishers
A Ministry of Bethany Fellowship, Inc.
11300 Hampshire Avenue South
Minneapolis, Minnesota 55438

Printed in the United States of America.

Library of Congress Cataloging-in-Publication Data

Tomlinson, Paul, 1940–
     How a man handles conflict at work / Paul Tomlinson.
          p. cm. —(Lifeskills for men)
     ISBN 1–55661–896–4
          1. Conflict management.   2. Male employees.   3. Life skills.
I. Title. II. Series.
HD42.T65   1996
158.2'6—dc21   96–45785
                                                                        CIP

To the great guys in my life,
to my wife Jeanne,
and to my daughter Corrie,
who spent precious time in
the editing of this manuscript.

PAUL TOMLINSON is Principal of Career/Life Institute, is a corporate consultant, and also provides individual and career assessments for teens, professionals, and executives. He holds a master's degree in psychology. He and his wife, Jeanne, live in Washington and have three children.

Acknowledgments

I have had more than my share of men in my life who have modeled for me the integration of biblical principles and their vocation. These men have found significance in their God and their work and have managed to put the two together in a way that seems natural. My goal has been to pass on to others what they have invested in me. My "Hall of Fame" includes:

Judge Tom Glover, then a fledgling attorney, introduced me to Christianity. Beyond the introduction was a discipling, mentoring relationship in which Tom invested his time in me.

Dr. Charles "Chuck" Dohner has been my prayer partner and mentor. His willingness to share his wisdom has been a blessing that has influenced and changed my life forever.

Zeke Easley, a now retired senior manager with IBM in Seattle, held a Bible study every Friday morning for a large group of business people. As a new believer, I attended his Friday morning group and saw that *real* men experienced the same conflicts I did. I also saw them turn to the Bible, God, and each other for support and answers.

Chuck Snyder is an advertising executive, author, and the grandfather with "the world's greatest grandkids." He demonstrated to me how to walk through the workday focused on God and others, while providing quality work to clients.

Bill Levings, a man of faith and integrity, handled the rigors of growing a small consulting business with grace and dignity. I worked for him for eight years. Even with numerous challenges, Bill kept people and ethics first while making decisions with dispatch.

Ralph Davidson, my father-in-law, taught me the value of making quality decisions and how to enjoy life along with work. Working for him as he remodeled our house, I learned that quality took a little more time (frustrating for me then) but that excellence was worth the wait. Full of energy and wisdom, Ralph has been, and is, an inspiration.

Babe Tomlinson, my dad, did two things for me. He gave me a strong ethical base for facing life, and he showed me how to be optimistic. Dad didn't make a lot of money, but he always had a smile on his face, was loyal to the company, and worked hard.

With all of the input from the men above, I would be remiss if I did not thank Jeanne, my wife, and mother to our three kids, who has taught me about love and dedication. Her support in my different adventures has been unswerving, and in some of our tough decisions, her battle cry has been, "Do you trust God or not?"

Contents

Introduction

Luke sat in front of me with his head down. He had just expressed a despondent feeling about his work that I have heard from so many men I've worked with in my career-counseling business.

A credit manager in a production facility, Luke's interpersonal relations in the office had been less than satisfactory. His stormy relationship with his "inefficient and blowhard" boss resulted in his popping antacid pills by the handful. He hated his job and had contemplated leaving many times over the years. He often felt guilty taking his paycheck because the work was easy and he didn't put much energy or enthusiasm into his job. Now he had just been told that he was being laid-off in four weeks, and at age forty-five, he was full of anguish.

For the last five years, Luke had become increasingly frustrated as conflict with people around him escalated. His attitude made him short-tempered at home, and he was "a little angry at God, too." But now that he felt his job slipping away—and with it, his family's security—he was alternately gripped by anger, fear, and an emotional exhaustion that left him depleted.

It would take us a while to sort out Luke's feelings, what he'd done to contribute to his present circumstances—*and* to bring hope back to the situation. It would take some simple training in conflict-resolving skills, in wise life/career management, and an honest look at Luke's attitudes—which he often conveyed to his boss and co-workers without even knowing it. Eventually, Luke was on-track again, mainly because he was willing to be honest and to make changes in his life and approach to work.

As a career and management consultant, I have worked with many men like Luke. Lethargy. Confusion. Fear. Anger. Guilt. These are only a few of the emotions that men experience when facing conflict related to their jobs. Yet conflict is inevitable. We grow and change in our interests. We feel stuck because of circumstances. And conflict comes with the territory when we work around other people. Even if you work alone in a cave or in a room with your trusty computer, there are still plenty of sources for inner conflict. My purpose in writing this book is to offer ideas for managing job-related strains in a direct, healthy manner, because I've yet to meet another man who doesn't face some fairly significant conflict related to his work.

It's my hope that what I've experienced, both as a manager and a consultant/counselor, will encourage you to tackle some of the stressors and problems you may be facing. Maybe what I've learned in working with over 5,000 people facing career and personal crises will bring you some insight. I will also share some of my personal experiences of victory and defeat.

I once was interviewed by an aspiring young consultant, and he asked me how I had done so well at my job.

"Two words—" I said, "*good decisions.*"

He looked puzzled. "How did you learn to make good decisions?"

"Experience," I told him.

"Well then, how did you get this experience?"

"Two words—" I answered, "*bad decisions.*"

Of course I was repeating an old story for this young guy, but the point is valid. You and I *will* gain some of our best experience through trial and error—*if* we are willing to learn and to keep moving our lives and careers in a positive direction.

You may be one of the fortunate ones who enjoys most aspects of his vocational life—the type of work, the pay, the growth or travel opportunities. Yet there may be one area of irritation, like a sliver in your finger. It might be a boss, or a co-worker, who constantly annoys you. Maybe you just want to have freedom to speak about your faith with others but struggle because you fear negative consequences.

I Need Help!

One reason I can relate to guys like Luke is because I've experienced the turmoil they have. Unemployed and confused, I faced a major crossroad in my life at the age of forty. I had just been asked to take a demotion from a senior management position and, after prayerful consideration, had resigned. I'd worked for big companies all my life and wasn't sure what I wanted. I did know a return to big corporate America was not on the list.

Starting my own consulting business was a possibility, but I didn't know if I had what it would take to make it work. Even though I'd left the organization by mutual consent, I had some insecurities and some doubts about my abilities. We didn't have a lot of cash in reserve, so I felt under pressure to come up with something quickly. I sought advice from several friends and prayed that I would find a satisfying and productive place to spend my time.

Over time, I began to get an impression that repeated it-self whenever I prayed. I felt that I should take all that I'd learned about corporate life and use it to help others find their way through job snafus. As I took steps to follow this new sense of direction, I moved into a consulting business where I indeed have served people for the last sixteen years.

Every day now, I work with some man who is facing a major conflict at work. My objective is to pinpoint the na-ture of the problem—not always as easy as you might think—and then to describe some of the causes and provide practical suggestions for resolving the conflict. Life is too short to be living in constant tension, defeat, bitterness, or unhappiness. I have chosen to address certain major stresses because I encounter them over and over again. Do any of these ring true for you?

- an unfair boss who is making your life miserable;
- a female co-worker who is tempting you to cross the line even though you're married;
- negative, critical co-workers who complain all the time and are dragging you down with them;
- lack of interest in a boring job with no room for ad-vancement;
- the pressures of deadlines and recent downsizings find you compromising integrity and lying about small mis-takes;
- peer pressure for you to slow down so others don't look bad or so you can charge a higher hourly rate—pressure to compromise quality or to cover for others' mistakes;
- fear of leaving your current, secure job for that position you have always dreamed about;
- ongoing tension with co-workers or customers.

The Wider Impact of Unresolved Conflict

Unresolved conflict at work can cause problems in other areas of our lives. I went through a period of turmoil caused by struggles with an insensitive boss. I discovered later that there was a negative residual effect on Jeanne and the kids. At home I wasn't "up," I had a tendency to be preoccupied, and—as they tell me now—I was "not much fun to be around."

When major frustrations loom over us, they influence the quality of our work and the intimacy of our relationships. They can also impact our health, physically and emotionally. Maybe we stop exercising, or pull away from friends and church, as we become increasingly frustrated or bitter. My desire, having been there, is to bring some insight and hope for you who are experiencing some of these conflicts.

Throughout the following chapters, I want you to know that you will see some recurring themes. These are key issues that will become the basis for resolving job conflicts. Look for these as you read:

- Problem identification (Is it my problem or theirs?)
- Confronting problems head-on (They'll only get worse if you don't.)
- Trusting God.
  Accountability (Learning to be open, honest, and prayerful with another man.)
- Anticipation (Expecting God to help and direct you in every situation.)

Two Sources of Conflict

Before we start, though, I want to be clear about one thing. We usually think of conflict as being caused by someone or something *outside* ourselves. But many times we

face frustration because of internal conflicts. Take Luke as
an example.

External. Luke was having trouble with relationships
with his co-workers and his boss. I had to determine
whether they were at fault or whether Luke had some blind
spots that were contributing to the problems. We found a
little of each. Luke had some very annoying habits, and his
boss needed a personality transplant! Ongoing conflict
with people is the primary source of external conflicts.

Internal. Luke had been unable to make a decision to
leave his job. So he remained torn inside between *security*
(and boredom) and *risk* (and excitement). This was a huge
source of conflict, and his attitude had gone steadily down-
hill for several years. Luke had made a commitment to follow Christ and live as a Christian early in his life, but he'd
gradually become a "Sunday only" Christian. He felt sep-
arated from God because he'd also come close to having an
affair with a married co-worker, which created additional
turmoil.

A large majority of the men I work with are dealing with
internal battles of confidence, guilt, and fear. The first step
out of your conflict is to take time to honestly, carefully
identify the true source or sources of the conflicts you are
facing. This will include taking a good look inward.

Dealing With Conflict

In my life I have used both the *knee-jerk* reaction and
the *head-in-the-sand* approach to solving job conflicts. It's
easy to hope that if you just ignore the problem it will go
away. These very human responses seldom work. Rarely do
problems go away by themselves. Nor can you rely on others to solve your problems. Luke's tensions began to resolve
the minute he saw he was not a victim but rather had control over many things he'd felt were someone else's fault or
responsibility. When he was able to see he had a problem

with communication and took steps toward change, he was surprised to find that others suddenly were much easier to get along with. No, he did not become best friends with his difficult boss. But he was able to establish a cordial working relationship for the time he had left on that job.

We are not the pawns of circumstance or other people. There *is* something you can do to improve a bad work situation, even if you did not cause it. And, as a Christian, I can assure you that God honors those who seek Him and who look for His help in every situation, as well as those who are willing to do the work that change requires. Many of us are in a rut. We put up with conflict because change is too risky. Getting out of our rut requires resolving conflict and moving on to the next growth step. It means letting go of old ways of thinking and acting, and taking responsibility for our own maturity and work needs.

I will not tell you that one answer "fits all." That's impossible, because God has designed us uniquely and we have different natural patterns for how we deal with conflict, change, and communication. My good friend Spike loves to tackle situations head-on. Over the years he's had to learn to slow down a bit. I prefer to analyze and postpone any action. I have had to learn to speed up and confront problems more promptly. The point is to learn what new living skills you need to help you make the right changes in your life.

I Need a Co-Pilot—So Do You

On a commercial airline, regulations require that there always is a co-pilot flying with the captain. This is because there are so many things to do, and instruments to check to keep the plane on-course. As you and I travel on the flight-path of life, many of us would like to do it solo. We may have asked God to play a role in our lives—but the truth is, we usually want to have Him sitting back in the passenger cabin. That way, we can pilot the ship and call on Him in case of emergency, or when we need a miracle. But God wants to be right up there in the cockpit with us, giving us the constant course-corrections it takes to navigate a life and a career. Every act of our work and life is part of God's business. If we wait to call upon Him until there's a crisis of major proportions—such as when we lose our job, or when we've been passed over for a promotion—we lose the benefit of having had godly counsel every step of the way.

We need to have an active, daily relationship with God in prayer—and *then* we can experience His presence and guidance when we confront problems. At one point in my life, I had a boss who was a source of tremendous conflict for me. I prayed a long time for *him* to change. But the way God's voice came to me was through my wife, who gave me very specific instructions for how *I* needed to change! I heeded Jeanne's words, and changed both my attitudes and my actions toward this manager. Today, many years later, we are good friends. Jeanne and I had a chance to be a part of the process in which he and his wife and four children made decisions to follow Christ. What a blessing we might have missed if I had left that job without resolving our conflict!

You see, God is not a prayer-answering machine. God wants to be involved in your life and personal growth. Jim is a man I know who had a problem with lying to cover his mistakes on the production line. I challenged him to ask God for strength to deal with his fear of failure. It meant his growing in maturity enough to look his boss in the eye and say, "I misread the tolerance on the specifications. It won't happen again."

When Jim began to take responsibility for his actions, he was on his way to becoming a man of personal integrity, and to finding fulfillment in his work. The good news is that God doesn't expect us to get out of the rut, confront others, or leave a dead-end job all under our own strength. In 2 Corinthians, we find His promise to us: "My grace is sufficient for you, for My strength is made perfect in weakness" (12:9, NKJV).

God *will* help you resolve your greatest conflicts at work, and the way He'll do it is to help you walk through key issues that can hinder you from growing as a man.

Accountability

Throughout the book, you will find reference to an "accountability partner." Chuck is a guy I've met with for prayer, discussion, and Bible study for twenty years. When schedules permit, we meet weekly—at other times, monthly. During our friendship, I've had three career moves, more than a few conflicts, and raised three children. We have talked about our faith and doubts, explored options to complicated problems at work—and *prayed* together. Chuck has been an invaluable resource to me professionally, spiritually, and emotionally. He is there to ask a probing question, to listen, to offer an observation, to critique my actions. And occasionally, to challenge me to get out of the rut of self-pity. It's taken guts.

Knowing of all the women I work with in my business, for instance, he once looked me in the eye and challenged me, "Are you keeping your relationships with the women you work with *pure?*" Fortunately, the answer was yes. It was a difficult question for him to ask, and I really appreciated his taking that specific risk to make sure I was on the straight-and-narrow. More than that, it gave me confidence to know I had a friend who cares enough to walk through hard places if need be. Chuck has helped keep me focused on godly living and has constantly called me back to the spiritual perspective. Chuck's friendship has also taken some of the pressure off Jeanne, because he has been another source of advice, and a place to express my anger—someone else to soften the effect of major disappointments.

I want to strongly encourage you to find a Christian friend with whom you can experience the support and challenge you need to grow as a man. With one or two others, you can be honest, ask the tough questions—or just get together and have a great relaxing time when the solution to problems is not yet apparent.

Remember, accountability is always a two-way street: Proverbs 27:17 says, "As iron sharpens iron, so one man sharpens another." Being able to support Chuck brought significance to my life as I prayed for his business and important decisions, and stood by him in the tough times. Having *both* God and Chuck as co-pilots has been an invaluable experience.

Your Work—God's Gift

I know that there is nothing better for men than to be happy and do good while they live. That everyone may eat and drink, and find satisfaction in all his toil—this is the gift of God (Ecclesiastes 3:12–13).

God has told us that work is a gift. Chuck Swindoll, in his book *Hand Me Another Brick*, tells about the Israelites rebuilding the wall around Jerusalem. When the wall was halfway up, they looked at how many bricks were left on the ground. Rather than praising God for what they'd accomplished, they looked at the work yet to be done and became discouraged. When surrounded by tough problems at work, it's tempting to focus on all you have left to do, rather than the progress you have already made.

There is one word that encourages me more than any other in our language—*hope*. Many men ask me, "Is there any hope of finding a solution to my situation?" The answer is always—*yes!* there is a way through your problem (and *no*, the light at the end of the tunnel is not an oncoming train!) Here are some Scriptures that encourage me:

- "For I know the plans I have for you . . . plans to prosper you and not to harm you, plans to give you hope and a future" (Jeremiah 29:11).
- "God is faithful; he will not let you be tempted beyond what you can bear" (1 Corinthians 10:13).
- "For God did not give us a spirit of timidity, but a spirit of power, of love and of self-discipline" (2 Timothy 1:7).
- "Be strong and courageous. Do not be terrified; do not be discouraged, for the Lord your God will be with you wherever you go" (Joshua 1:9).

God tells us that all His unlimited care, guidance, and resources are available to each one of us.

My prayer is that as you read this book you will increasingly focus on God and His Word before you act. This is the essence of Christian maturity and will go a long way toward easing any conflict in your life.

Conflict #1:
When You Hate
Your Job

In his book *Why America Doesn't Work*, Charles Colson describes experiments in a WW II German prison camp. Prisoners of war were told to move piles of heavy rocks in wheelbarrows from point A to point B. When they finished, they were told to move all the rocks back to point A again. This went on for days . . . weeks. The insignificance of the work drove some of the prisoners to a mental breakdown. My career coaching experience indicates that many men feel that in their work they are mindlessly "moving rocks," and going crazy.

Do you feel that you are adding something of value to life, to the world, with your work? Do you take pleasure most days in reviewing your accomplishments, knowing you've made a difference? If not—have you found a way to change your situation? One of the major conflicts men face at work comes when they feel they are not making a contribution, that their work has little or no value, that they are engaged in mindless insignificant activity.

Same Ol', Same Ol'

Many men find themselves in careers that lack purpose. They may feel trapped as each boring day repeats itself over and over.

If you hate your job, you may be missing two key ingredients—*passion* and *significance*.

Friends, life is too short to have protracted periods of just "moving rocks," or going through the motions at work. For sure, there will be times for all of us when work isn't that exciting. But internal conflict arises when passion and significance are absent for an extended period of time. Escaping this trap calls for action on two fronts: *First*, you can begin to define what passion and significance mean to you; *second*, you can take steps to bring these two necessary components into your life.

John, a professional at an international software company, came to me urgently seeking help. He was performing well, and the nature of the work was generally to his liking—but inside, a sort of "deadness" was numbing him. As he explained, "I have no fire in my belly. I have no drive and my work has no meaning." John wondered if there wasn't more to work than what he was experiencing. His conflict was that people were lined up for a job like his, and yet he had no feelings of passion for what he was doing. His question to me was, "Is there something wrong with me?"

What Is Passion?

Men with *passion* look forward to the relationships and responsibilities that await them at work. The man with passion awakens to the day's activities with positive thoughts: "Bring 'em on, I can't wait to get to the challenges of the day!" He feels anticipation for the work to be done, the decisions to be made, and the problems to be solved. Instead of feeling passion, perhaps you are waking up with a heavy heart—even blaming God for your situation. How about it? Do you look forward to your day at work with enthusiasm, or dread?

Here are some reasons why passion for work may be missing:

- *Failure to identify what's important in a career.* Maybe you have never taken the time to clarify what's important to help you progress vocationally, hoping that someday the right job, the right opportunity, will miraculously appear.
- *Poor experience in past work situations.* You have no hope that your current situation will be any better.
- *You didn't know having passion for work was possible.* Most people you know think of work as something you do whether you like it or not.

The Move Toward Significance

The term *significance* assumes that what we do is important and has meaning for ourselves and others. A man's work gives him significance when, at the end of a day or week, he can say, "I made a difference!" Life takes on a good measure of meaning and purpose when we make a contribution to a task, or to other people.

Don is the owner of a repair business, and is now semi-retired. He doesn't want to give up his work entirely, he says, because "my work gives me such a good feeling. When someone calls with a major appliance that's not working, and I appear at their house, they're glad to see me. And when I have it working again, I feel an incredible sense of accomplishment." Don is describing his mode of finding significance in his work.

Why Significance Is Absent

Here are some reasons why a sense of contribution can be lacking:

- *Failure to identify what's personally rewarding.* Perhaps you have not taken time to define what it is that you consider to be significant.
- *Feeling inadequate, unworthy.* Some men feel that they are incapable of making a contribution that's worthwhile.
- *Not understanding God's definition of significance.* Making a contribution from God's perspective differs from the general view that says we need to achieve position, power, prestige, and respect from many people. If you don't understand significance from God's perspective, you will struggle with personal significance at work.

If any of these issues are confronting you now, meet with a trusted friend to begin sorting out your thoughts about significance and purpose in your work. What gives you a sense of accomplishment? What do you want to do to make a difference? Where do you need to be working—if it's not the job you're in now—in order to bring interest and vitality into your life?

Related Areas of Conflict

I have discovered in working with men that when we feel a lack of passion and significance, our level of frustration builds up easily. Can you see yourself in any of the following examples?

- Ben's relationship at home, at work, and with friends became strained. He didn't talk much in the first place, but having a job that didn't fire him up made him close off even more. His frustrations began to rip apart his relationship with his wife.

- Karl was active in church youth work—but his responsibilities at work had diminished so much that, in his
  mind, he was no longer making a significant contribution. He had worked so hard, and he didn't deserve to
  feel degraded. He slowly cut back his youth work and
  told a trusted friend, "Look at me. How can I tell anyone
  about God, or how great it is to be a Christian, when I
  feel like my life stinks?"
- Randy had lost his zeal for his construction job. And
  now the quality and quantity of his work was far below
  his old standard. "What's the use? I just put in my
  time." His boss was unwilling to expand into new areas
  of construction, so there was no drive to learn more or
  to improve his performance.
- Bryan put on fifty pounds when he failed to be promoted to police lieutenant. He stopped exercising and
  lost his motivation to eat healthy foods. When it came
  to personal appearance, he thought, *Who cares?*

What's at the Root?

Most men want to feel that their work makes a difference. When we work day after day and believe our work is
valueless, an internal conflict results. On one hand stands
the reality of our situation, and on the other stands our
dreams and personal expectations. If you are at this point,
you need to take a serious look at your career direction.
Three situations can occur:

Passion Without Significance
    On numerous occasions I've consulted with men who
feel an affinity for their work, but feel no significance.
Workers in three industries come to mind immediately: oil,
lumber, and banking. Technology, market conditions, and
staff reductions have changed the nature of these indus-

tries. One group of Northwest timber managers loved the scope and responsibility of the business, but they had become discouraged over the diminished logging operations. Career-wise, there was no room to grow or expand their work. They felt as if they were treading water, and their work had no apparent meaning.

Have you been in a job you loved, but now find yourself demoted, transferred, or reassigned to a new position? Inner conflict can occur when new duties fail to provide the same level of satisfaction. What can you do? Three options are: find a new position within the industry; accept the new status and reexamine your definition of personal significance; leave the company or industry. I can point to successful examples of all three approaches.

Significance Without Passion

Computer technicians, scientists, company owners, mechanics, and tool-and-die professionals have come to my office—all having problems with jobs others would love to have. They're often making good money and are contributing to the mission of their group, but their interest, desire, and emotion have dissipated. Each one makes basically the same statement: "A lot of people think I'm crazy for wanting to leave the good thing I've got going. Some guys would die to have my job!"

Jim was an engineering project manager for a large firm, and in the past he'd successfully designed several infrastructure systems that led to significant profits and had made other major contributions to the organization. Without warning, he lost all desire for the work, the numbers, and the industry. Although Jim felt significance, without passion his job was no longer enjoyable.

Jim's problem was his type-A personality and his high energy level. Men who have high energy and great confidence in their skills often become restless and feel the need to move on. Some may adjust to their situation, learn to be content, and stay. But those who stay and continue to moan that work is "no fun" are difficult to be around.

How about you? Is this basic drive the cause of your restlessness? Do you need to come to terms with the fact that you're a high-energy, short interest-span kind of guy—and learn to cope with it?

No Significance or Passion

When both of these factors are absent, you have a major problem!

Paul was a pastor with fifteen years invested in his ministry. The congregation had not grown, and people were complaining about the lifeless church programs. As we talked, he lamented, "Is it me, or is it the congregation?" He hated looking at his "to do" list. Was the problem his lack of fire? Was the lack of growth in the congregation *cause*, or *effect*? He also wondered if there were other issues involved—such as competence level, personal credibility, commitment, even simple people skills or lack thereof. Eventually, Paul resigned as senior pastor and became an assistant pastor in a larger church, where he found great satisfaction in serving without the constant burden of leadership. Which is to say, he found his solution by examining the *role* he had fallen into, which did not suit him.

Men, there are various reasons why we can wind up in the wrong roles, in the wrong jobs. Someone told us we'd be good at a certain calling, when it didn't suit us at all. We thought we'd enjoy a better salary, or more prestige, or just personal enjoyment—only to find out the job role did not suit us at all.

To change roles—whether in the same general line of work, like Paul, or to another line of work—takes guts. But if there is a chance to find work you can do with passion and a sense of significance, isn't it worth the risk?

When Passion and Significance Are Present

Men who experience the ideal in their work and believe they are making a contribution will possess most or all of the following benefits:

- They have a sense of being in God's will.
- They believe that God is a partner in their activity.
- Time moves quickly.
- Energy is abundant, and they don't readily get tired.
- There is a sense of being "in the groove."
- Their reward is in the effort itself. (They don't need a lot of ego strokes.)
- There is a sense of being in control.
- Fear and anxiety are absent. (Problems are seen as challenges, not obstacles.)

Don was working in a low-paying sales job, with bosses watching his every move and pushing him to higher and higher quotas. At fifty, he was experiencing all of the frustrations associated with the absence of passion or significance and came to me looking for help. We reviewed in detail Don's interests, motivations, and skills. The career-planning exercises he completed revealed that he

- desired to work with his hands, making and repairing items;
- would like to serve and work with people;
- wanted freedom to move around and not have strict supervision.

For Don, serving others and using some strong technical skills that his sales job didn't require were the basic elements of a perfect job. We prayed that God would direct his path.

Don eventually started his own repair and preventive maintenance business, working with restaurants, nursing homes, and mobile home parks. He never thought that he

could put his interests, motivations, and skills together to
have what he desired. Today he is enjoying both passion
and significance in his career. With God, *all things are possible!*

Getting Passion Into Your Work
    One of the first things I ask men is this: "What is the
perfect job, or the elements of a perfect job, for you right
now?" Fifty percent have difficulty answering that question initially. Some Christian men even wonder if it isn't
selfish to set your own goals or career path. After all,
shouldn't you be asking God to give you your life's plan?
Yes, you should—but He often does so by helping us use
the abilities He gave us at birth. As Psalm 37:4, says,
"Delight yourself in the Lord, and He will give you the desires of your heart." Finding God's direction for your career
need not require a mystical revelation. It can be as natural
as understanding the desires He has already built into you.
A passion for God *will* give us energy to pursue the other
passions in our life.
    On the other hand, some of our difficulty in finding passion in our work is that we can put too much emphasis on
the work and not enough on God. Delighting in the Lord
requires personal prayer time, fellowship with other believers, reading the Word, and asking God to help remove
sin from our lives. I believe that a new passion comes when
we open up to God and allow His to direct us into meaningful work that connects us to people, to services, and to
life in a way that stirs our deepest emotions.

The Desire of Our Heart

    Research indicates that many men form a vision or mental picture about their career in their teens, and then seek
to fulfill that dream. The dream can be clear and specific—

physician, truck driver, missionary, carpenter. It can also be broad in scope—own a business, travel, have success and wealth. Later in life, many men find that their original vision is no longer valid. Is that true for you? Perhaps you've found that your heart's desire is unattainable—say, to be a fighter pilot, but your eyesight is not 20/20. Perhaps you've outgrown your original vision but have never replaced it with another.

In the movie *Mr. Holland's Opus*, Richard Dreyfus plays a man who aspires to be a composer of orchestral music but "settles" for being a high school music teacher. He continues to dream and does great work with the students, but is never really satisfied with his role. What he accomplishes as a music teacher is significant, but he doesn't fully enjoy the fruits of his labor. Along the way, he failed to switch his vision from composer to educator.

Living with passion requires us to define the desire of our heart, and then to follow that desire until God says, *yes, no*, or *I have something better.*

How to Build a Dream

Are you in a place where you need to redefine your dream and vision? If so, take time to identify the components of your perfect job:

- Write out your past accomplishments at work, home, church, in the community. Look at what you have most enjoyed in these activities.
- What are your interests—people, things, writing, speaking, numbers, recreation, or some combination of these?
- What are the motivations that bring value to your work—to lead, serve, research, bring order out of chaos, negotiate or sell, to educate others?
- What skills do you have—mechanical or construction abilities, computers, verbal or written communication,

driving, listening, management, negotiating, sales, problem-solving?

In analyzing your interests, motivations, and skills, areas of passion will begin to materialize. You may want to read a book on careers,[1] call a career counselor, or meet with some other men and discuss what really pushes your "hot button." Ask God to reveal where you should be. Make no mistake, this is a process in which you must actively take part.

Make the Dream Big Enough to Involve God

Whether you're still chasing the dream of your youth or building a new one, the dream should be bigger than what you can accomplish alone. If you can make the dream happen by yourself, who needs God? The desire of my heart was to have a part-time ministry which would be supported by work in the business world. This seemed impossible. But a few months after defining this vision, I was approached by the owner of a career business who said he would teach me the profession and send me to college for a Master's Degree. I told him my ideal mix of work was three days of consulting and two days of ministry, and he agreed to that plan. The dream was beyond what I could have imagined, and I gave God credit for the result.

I offer this caution: There is a difference between stepping out in faith and taking a foolish risk that puts your family in financial jeopardy. A step of faith is undertaken prayerfully and with input from trusted advisors. One of the best ways to distinguish between these two, if you are married, is to ask your wife. I have made four career moves in my life, and each one took me outside my comfort zone. Each time I have discovered the faithfulness, love, and support of a God who cares personally for me as He does for you.

I want to encourage those of you living without a passion—*build a vision for work.* I know that you will develop the first glimmers of passion for work again.

How important is this simple first step?

Psychologists say that people have at least two basic needs: the need to love and be loved, and the need to know that what we are doing is significant. In some way, we all either want our work to benefit others directly or we want to be an important part of a team effort. Making a contribution involves *more than what we do.* That is a shallow measure if that is all we use to gauge significance. In order to find *true* significance, we must have a balance between three areas: what we do, who we are, and Whose we are. Without a fine interworking of all three components we'll have conflict and frustration.

What I Do

When our work is significant, we will experience most of the following:

You will have a personal sense of making a contribution. Ken took pleasure in doing financial planning for his customers. At the end of most every day, he could look back and say, "I made a difference."

You will experience identification with your value base—that is, living in a way that reflects what's important to you. Roy left an excellent job with a beverage distributor. The responsibility and pay were outstanding, but he could not personally reconcile distribution of beer and wine with his Christian principles.

You will sense your value to others. My uncle was a taxi driver in Los Angeles. He experienced both passion and significance because he knew he added value to the lives of the people he transported, talked with, and encouraged.

You will have a sense of being in God's will. In starting

my current business in the early '90s, I believed the work to be done was part of God's will for my life at that time. I had prepared well and prayed diligently. Jeanne and I felt at peace, even though I was leaving a high-paying job and had two kids in college at the time.

Who I Am

Bill was like many other men I've known—myself included. His definition of significance was in his accomplishments, getting recognition from others, and in holding a high position in the company. In his mind, personal significance was based almost solely on *performance*.

Bill came to me as a very distraught young man of thirty-two who had just been fired from a high-level hospital post. He had never failed until then, and his reaction was highly emotional. Together we discovered that he defined who he was *entirely* by what he did in his work. Therefore, the termination was especially devastating.

After a painful process of self-examination, he took a job with lower pay and less responsibility—and yet he has felt both passion and significance return. Understanding who he is *apart from his job* allowed him to find a career that better fit his God-given design.

The following is a partial list of words that may help you to define yourself as person apart from what you do to earn a living. You may want to place a check mark by those that reflect who you are.

☐ Kind   ☐ Competent   ☐ Faithful
☐ Compassionate ☐ Loving   ☐ Peaceful
☐ Committed   ☐ Curious   ☐ Christ-
☐ Independent   ☐ Persistent   centered
☐ Caring

Whose I Am

At the age of thirty-two, I came to believe in God as Creator and in Jesus as my Savior. In time, I realized that my real value and significance was founded in God's love and sacrifice for me. Every man—from the just-released federal prisoner washing dishes in a new job to the company president—has significance because of *Whose* they are, not because of what they do.

I have significance because of Whose I am. And so do you if you have surrendered your life to God in Christ.

Because we belong to God, we can rest assured that God sometimes uses times of dryness, conflict, or struggle to get our attention. If we seek His guidance, these times will refocus us and get us ready for what He has for us next. One such time caused me to redefine what was significant to me: serving people; leveraging my knowledge through teaching and coaching; spreading the Good News; and helping Christians mature in their faith. That led to starting my own business and also setting up a non-profit Christian ministry—which is what occupies me today.

No matter how devoid of passion you may feel right now, no matter how great your hunger for significance, I can promise you: God will redirect your steps, guiding you into the work that fulfills the desires of your heart—*if* you take time to pray, examine your heart, and seek the guidance of other men.

Frederick Buechner has said it best: "The place God calls you to is the place where your deep gladness and the world's deep hunger meet."

For Thought and Discussion

1. Is your work significant in your eyes at this time? If not, are you ready to do something about it?
2. Are you in the right career, but needing a different job to maximize your talents and God-given design? Or is a career change necessary in order for you to maximize your talents and God-given design?

3. Do you base your value on what you do, or who you are? Do you understand your relationship to God well enough to let Him guide you and open the way to necessary changes?

Note

1. See the Bibliography at the back of the book.

Conflict #2: Stuck in a Dead-End Job

Jeff knew there were risks when he took the job with his best friend's family-owned lumber business. They promised that if he learned the operations from the ground up, he'd be rewarded with a minority ownership and be a key member of management. Jeff worked hard, learned to price wood products, and to drive the forklift. He made sales calls and heard, "You're doing great!" But . . .

Fifteen months later, he was still in the yard "learning" his trade, with the same pay, empty promises, and more than a little anger. Jeff found it difficult to get up and go to work only to face the same routine he'd learned months ago. His motivation was low, and his dream of ownership was rapidly fading. Jeff was experiencing one of the conflicts many men find at work. His job was at a dead end, and he was having a serious bout of lethargy.

Art was the owner of a small landscaping firm. As he looked halfheartedly at the bills, he pondered the impact of his competition and declining profitability. Staring over his third cup of coffee, he wondered, "Is this really worth it?"

The thought of the day's activities—training employees, calling on a new customer, solving a nasty complaint from a large vendor—had Art frozen. He didn't have enough capital to expand. Where was there to go? Something between deadness and despair gripped his chest.

Have you ever been at a point where your job looked like a dead end? When it happens, a man can be overwhelmed with the thought of a future that looks bleak. I speak from personal experience, having hit this career brick wall a couple of times myself. And I've frequently encountered this very common area of job conflict with many, many other men.

Hitting the Wall

If you are not there already, it's likely that at some point during the course of your career, some of the following events will cause you to feel like you're going nowhere:

- boredom with routine work;
- a boss, or owner, who brings in a friend or family member for a position for which you are qualified—and wanted;
- no pay increase or a reduction in pay;
- passed over for promotion;
- forced to work 10–20 hours overtime each week or lose your job;
- the broken promise of a supervisor in regard to training, or a new job;
- personal or family-related health concerns that make you feel you *can't* leave a go-nowhere position;
- knowing that this job is not a good fit, the company is not right, or that you don't have the skills it would take to get ahead;
- a fast-changing environment that's disorganized, with

too much management or personnel turnover to get the job done without constant hassle.

If you don't resolve these frustrations, the internal conflict will drive you crazy! I was there in my early thirties. As a middle manager in a bank, I saw no future in my job, was cynical about my managers, and didn't like the work or the structure of a large organization. I felt like I was dead-ending, and my negative attitude began to impact my life both in the office and at home. The thought of going to work in the morning gave me a heavy feeling in the pit of my stomach. I was experiencing the physical, emotional, and relational impacts of lethargy.

Lethargy and Apathy

Matt was a commodities broker in the midst of marital problems—and then he was told that a less-qualified employee had been promoted over him. His secretary began complaining about Matt's lack of sensitivity. As conflicts mounted, Matt stayed in his office and withdrew from most contact with others. Many of us have felt that urge but have dutifully moved ahead into tasks and relationships. Matt, however, was in an advanced stage of lethargy.

When we feel trapped in a dead end, our disposition and attitude changes dramatically. Some men are geared to fight and take the conflict head on, while others of us try to ignore or run from the situation. Whether you are an employee or business owner, you can experience frustration that can lead to debilitating lethargy . . . and then to apathy.

Lethargy is a state of inaction—or a feeling that you *cannot* act. It's like a weight on your whole being. It can be a fleeting condition—a few hours or days. Or it can be with you every waking moment. Jeff, Art, and Matt were all experiencing lethargy. None of them felt like taking action to make a plan that would change his situation. The man with lethargy says, "I'm a little out of focus. I want to get back on course but I'm not sure how." When lethargy moves in, it's like a dull, gray, cold fog. It begins almost without notice, slowly becoming part of your awareness and then enveloping you. Concentration is painful, hope is dimmed, and life loses its sparkle. Lethargy is not a respecter of persons. It strikes all income levels, moves across racial and gender lines, impacts union workers as well as executives, those with years of education as well as high school dropouts.

As it progresses, lethargy can turn into *apathy*, which is a complete lack of passion, emotion, or excitement—even indifference to what normally appeals to your feelings or interests. At the point of apathy, a man's common response is, "I don't know and I don't care." At worst, prolonged lethargy and apathy can cause physical problems and lead to clinical depression—all the more reason to deal with it quickly when it arises.

Telltale Signs of Lethargy
    Carefully read some of the signs that can help you determine if you've reached a dead end and lethargy is taking over:

- Inability to clarify thoughts, to plan, think creatively, or focus; mind may wander, daydream.
- Free-floating frustration—with projects, with relationships, and with getting work done.
- Pressure associated with deadlines or too much work makes you feel physically, emotionally, or spiritually depleted.
- Stacking and restacking papers; doing the same work over.
- Temper flares more easily; annoyance with others increases.

- Anxiety and worry. Sleeplessness.
- Desire to pull away from relationships at work; avoid coffee breaks, lunches with co-workers; extroverts may go the other direction and increase talking to avoid work.
- Anger (or bitterness) directed at one or more people at work, which may erupt in thoughts during off-hours.
- Increase in spur-of-the-moment decisions just to get things done.
- Physical discomfort and worry; accident proneness.
- Quality and quantity of work has slipped below previously held standards; work is not getting done.
- You don't really care about productivity and outcomes.
- You have a negative attitude in your personal life.

If you have even two or three of these in your life at the same time, I sympathize with you because you are dealing with a high level of frustration. Being unable to move ahead is confusing to any man—especially the Christian man who may think there is something wrong with his faith. Lethargy and apathy can overtake anyone, so don't be too quick to judge or criticize a man who is suffering with these symptoms, including yourself. If you are experiencing traits on this list, it's a call to *action*. The way out requires a combination of planning, discipline, guidance from God, and action.

Working Out of Lethargy

Having worked with hundreds of men experiencing dead-end jobs and lethargy, I know that there are specific actions you can take to find a solution. And I know that you can ask God to enlarge your perspective on life, the job market, and *possibilities*. Proverbs 16:3 says, "Commit to the Lord whatever you do, and your plans will succeed." I know that means *new* plans, for a new start in your work.

A first step in getting out of your dead end is to clearly identify any underlying problems. Try to remember how long you've been in this condition. Check the following list:

- *A vocational issue.* Do you need a different job, more training or education?
- *An inability to deal with conflicts at work.*
- *Relationships.* Do you have an inability to get along with people? Is it that your management style doesn't work?
- *Motivation.* Is the drive to face and deal with issues missing?
- *Failure to achieve goals or financial targets.*
- *A personal problem*—finances, marriage, children, parents?
- *A physical problem*—headaches, illness, allergic reactions; need more exercise?
- *Fear*—of the unknown, the "information age," age creep?
- *Failure to move closer to God or to include Him in your problem solving.* Underneath it all, do you feel abandoned by God or angry at Him?
- Is God giving you a wake-up call to get your attention?

If any of these points speak to you, take the time to analyze your situation. Unless you take some action steps, you can be set up for moral and personal failure—an affair, recurring illness, loss of professional respect, lost business. Instead of facing the problem and looking for a solution, many men resign themselves to misery or try for an "instant fix"—a new car (or motorcycle), a new wardrobe, a new wife.

In the opening chapter, I told you about my friend Chuck, with whom I meet to pray and talk honestly. I've also prayed regularly with John and Spike. They've been invaluable to me in listening, offering suggestions, and

challenging my ideas. They pray with me and for me. Finding a man with a good listening ear is another important
step in walking out of a dead-end job. Fewer than 10 percent of the men who come to see me have even one other
man with whom they are open and honest. A Saturday
morning men's group at church, while important, is *not* my
definition of that relationship. Honesty and accountability
require an atmosphere of *safety*. Safety comes when there
is confidentiality, when men don't patronize each other or
act like know-it-alls.

When you meet with men, be clear as to your purpose.
Discuss the specific challenges that may be causing your
problem. The very act of expressing yourself is powerful. If
you don't air your thoughts to someone else, you'll probably hear them again and again, and the frustration, disap-
pointment, or anger will eat at you.

If you are married, you will most likely discuss the matter with your wife. Some men clam up entirely, and that's
a relationship killer. Some men dump their anger on their
wives, as if they were some kind of emotional dumping
ground. That's a bad idea too. The word here is *balance*.
Here is some simple advice: when you talk about major job
problems with your wife, try not to burden her every day
with all your heavy thoughts. Save the heavy stuff for your
friends or a counselor. Do share progress and ideas and ask
for her input on decisions. Your wife will know when
you've hit the wall and are frustrated—but don't make her
your only source of strength.

If your relationship with God is weak because of ne-
glect, there is no better time than now to begin anew. Express your need. Ask God to help you see yourself clearly.
Ask Him to guide you in what the next steps should be. As
you pray you may want to

- give thanks daily for what you have;

- confess your doubt, self-centeredness, or fear;
- ask God for specific answers for specific problems (relationships, focus, performance success, and career direction);
- read the Bible; such books as Joshua, Judges, Matthew, and James give encouragement and strength. The Psalms provide rest and peace, and can give you words to express emotions such as frustration and anguish;
- pray for God to reveal the sources of the frustration, if you really don't know what they are.

Personally, I like to lean on this promise: "The Lord is faithful to all his promises and loving toward all He has made. The Lord upholds all those who fall and lifts up all who are bowed down" (Psalm 145:13–14).

Goals—or Desires?

A big key to getting out of a dead end is learning what you can and cannot control. Some guys stay in nowhere jobs because they think they can pressure, leverage, or manipulate their boss or their circumstances. That's a formula for *unhealthiness*. To other men, work obstacles can seem overwhelming because they feel there is nothing they can do. Nonsense. A balanced approach to gaining control of your situation is a principle offered by counselor Larry Crabb. It involves understanding the difference between a desire and a goal.

A desire is something you want to have happen although you have no control over the final outcome: "I wish my boss would make up his mind and stick with a plan instead of being so scatterbrained." You can't control the boss or his weak management skills. If you make this *desire* into a *goal*—that is, setting out to change him—you are guaranteed both to fail and to become frustrated in the process.

A goal is something that you want to have happen and can to some degree control the outcome. A goal contains steps we can plan, implement, and measure. "I will find a time to tell the boss I would like more responsibility. I will carefully plan to make sure I do it in a positive manner." The meeting and presentation is your *goal*.[1] Bob was a retail store manager who had been at the same location for eight years. His career had plateaued and he was bored stiff. Then he heard of plans for a new company store across town. He told me, "I'm excited for the first time in months. I sure would like to be transferred to the new retail store opening in April. This decision is going to be made by two or three levels of management who will be considering several qualified candidates." His *desire* was to get the job, so he set *goals* that were within his control:

- He let his boss and the human resources department know of his desire to be transferred.
- He increased commitment to excellence in his current job.
- He reminded his manager of the skills he had to do the new, desired job.

Eric is another man who found a way out of his dead-end work. His boss was super-critical, took credit for some of Eric's efforts and ideas, and put him down in front of others. The boss's insensitivity and poor management style were definitely contributing to Eric's condition of lethargy and depression. Eric's *desire* was for a new boss or a new job, so he began to pray for a new position. He would have remained stuck in a terrible rut if he had tried to change his boss, because the man remained arrogant and abusive to the end.

Together we developed a set of *goals*—specific actions that Eric could take that might lead to the desired outcome. He was to

- treat the boss with respect, even if he didn't deserve it;
- stop complaining to others in the office;
- pray for his boss daily;
- evaluate his own work and reach for renewed excellence.

Even with the office atmosphere unchanged, Eric began working with a new sense of purpose. His energy returned, and within nine months he was offered a promotion to another department—with another boss. He also moved from despair to a new situation, which he saw as a miraculous gift from God.

When you're facing a dead end in your work, there may be many things that are beyond your control. As you determine to escape the onset of lethargy, here are some steps to take:

- Present your request to God in prayer. Give Him permission to change your desire, if necessary, by showing you what's best for you: "Lord, the desire of my heart is that new job. I offer this to you in case you have another plan. Show me."
- Ask other men to talk you through the situation and to pray for you.
- Make a commitment to take actions that you can control—setting measurable goals that might help the desire become reality.
- Ask for help from your friends or a counselor.

Those of us who confuse desires and goals—feeling that outcomes will somehow "just happen"—or fail to take action to determine those things we can control, are headed for ulcers and an emotional downward spiral. Achieving a goal requires active planning, action, and follow-through. It requires taking personal responsibility to act on what we can, leaving what we can't change or control to God.

How to Get Moving

Suppose you have determined that you have all the symptoms of lethargy. You've also decided that you need to do something. Perhaps you even have a list of what you need to do—but you just can't seem to *get going*. The following is a graphic example of the right and wrong ways to deal with this problem when the "dead-end-job blues" have a grip on you:

The Wrong Way
Positive Feelings = Actions = Results
    It's tempting to wait until you *feel* right to get going with your plan of action. You say things like

- "I'll start my plan when I feel better."
- "When my old drive comes back, then I'll find a friend to pray with."
- "I'll make those calls (or write that resumé) as soon as I have a little more energy."

Unfortunately, when those feelings don't come right away, the lethargy hangs on, because actions never get started. After a time, you sense that if something is going to happen, someone else is going to have to do it. Many men who operate like this find themselves pleading with God to make changes for them, or they hash their bad feelings over and over, with no resolution in sight.

Another Way
Actions = Results = Positive Feelings
    If you first take responsibility (actions), you will have

some success (results), which will lead to encouragement, hope, and awareness of God's activity in your life and career (positive feelings).

Here are some actions you can take even when you don't feel like it:

- Prioritize work assignments and begin to work on the most important project first. Write down targets and deadlines.
- Look for the positive in your life, no matter how bleak you feel. Keeping a larger perspective is key to a positive spirit and attitude.
- Increase work productivity and effectiveness. Work better and better each day.
- Get out of your shell and begin to make contact with co-workers and friends.
- Make an effort to resolve conflicts that may exist. Examine your own role in the conflict first. If necessary, confront others patiently without attacking. (And remember, you can't control their response to your best efforts!)
- Meet and pray with a trusted male friend. Find a mentor.
- Work on a plan that will identify the ideal job.
- Keep a prayer log book of requests and answers. Write down specific instances in which God has provided help.

There is no formula that will work in twenty-four hours, like taking a time-release capsule, but these steps have brought me and countless clients out of lethargy. It may take some assistance from people in your life who care, but be sure to follow through.

And give the transition some *time*.

Light at the End of the Tunnel

Larry, in his mid-thirties, saw the challenge in his job come to a halt. He held a lead position in the machine shop, but the time just seemed to drag by, and he had difficulty finding enough energy for the day. He withdrew from his co-workers and put in his eight hours halfheartedly. More and more he escaped from his family—into hunting, surfing the Internet, and endless hours of TV. He came through my door with a lot of inner turmoil and very little hope for the future.

Together we developed an active approach to get his work and life back on-track. In this case, Larry decided to make the best of it where he was until God provided something better. So he began to concentrate on performing his responsibilities to the best of his ability, and rebuilt communication with his co-workers. He began to pray and ask God to give him patience, but also asked for opportunities for a change. He established a relationship with a Christian mentor to talk through his plans and ideas.

Some months later, an upper-level manager took Larry aside and told him that he'd been noticing both his positive attitude and his excellent work. He mentioned the possibility of a promotion in the weeks ahead. During this period, as part of his action plan, Larry applied for other jobs, including a position in a ministry organization. After an extended interview process, he was offered a job. Prior to leaving, he was able to give his testimony to several top managers, explaining why ministry was his choice.

As Larry discovered, perhaps the biggest factor in getting out of a dead end comes when you determine to change your attitude. Then, when a change in circumstances comes, you are able to move on as a new person. Much of the process of lifting yourself out of the pit of lethargy has to do with personal change.

Here's some wisdom from Chuck Swindoll on that subject:

> The longer I live, the more I realize the impact of attitude on life. Attitude, to me, is more important than facts. It is more important than the past, than education, than money, than circumstances, than failures, than successes, than what other people think or say or do. It is more important than appearance, giftedness, or skill. It will make or break a company . . . a church . . . a home. The remarkable thing is we have a choice every day regarding the attitude we will embrace for that day. We cannot change our past . . . we cannot change the fact that people will act a certain way. We cannot change the inevitable. The only thing we can do is play on the one string we have, and this is our attitude. . . . I am convinced that life is 10 percent what happens to me and 90 percent how I react to it. And so it is with you . . . we are in charge of our attitudes.[2]

If you are in a dead-end job and the symptoms of lethargy have you paralyzed, remember—this is not some incurable disease. There is no value in self-pity. But there is value in humbling yourself before God and saying, "Help, I can't handle this by myself. Show me the way." Change your attitude, take action, trust God. And then watch Him provide a way out, to a new phase of your career and your life.

For Thought and Discussion

1. Are you in a dead-end job?
2. Are you experiencing signs of lethargy or apathy? Which ones?
3. List steps you will take to get yourself moving again.

Notes

1. For application of this principle in your marriage, see Law-
rence Crabb, Jr., *The Marriage Builder: A Blueprint for Couples
and Counselors* (Grand Rapids, Mich.: Zondervan Publishing
House, a Division of HarperCollins, 1992).
2. Chuck Swindoll, *Strengthening Your Grip* (Waco, Tex.: Word
Books, 1982) p. 206.

Conflict #3:
Should I Quit My Job?

Jake was a thirty-one-year-old guy who called me, sounding desperate for some immediate career counsel. He held a master's degree from a prestigious seminary and had once hoped to be a pastor. But during school he started working for a national express-packaging firm and was now making $36,000 a year. He had two children, some school debt, and a house payment. The desperation came from the fact that he deeply disliked his job—but a move into ministry would mean lower pay and that his wife might have to stop being an at-home mom and go to work. He felt trapped and could see no good way out without violating something he valued.

Should he leave his job for the sake of "meaning" and "personal fulfillment"—or stay for the sake of his family's security? He could serve God in other ways, after all, besides becoming a full-time pastor. How did he *know* what move to make, and whether he should leave his job to find satisfaction, or stay and find satisfaction in his current job?

I have listened to many stories like Jake's. Some men

have *had* it. Their jobs are terrible, and they're ready to "split now," willing to go anywhere and do anything to escape the unbearable nature of their current work situation.

Have you ever been so fed up with your job that you were ready to walk out? Maybe you're about to leave a job now, because you're being laid-off, or you're ready for that next career step. Whatever the case, leaving a job in the right way can mean the difference between a satisfying career change and continued frustration in your next position.

Hey, City Slicker, Is It Time for a Change?

In the movie *City Slickers*, actor Billy Crystal portrays a character who recognizes that he is getting older, and his career vision for the future is not clear. Missed opportunities haunt him. He's concerned about too much hair growing out of his ears, and too little on his head. His search for the next step in life, on a western cattle drive, struck a chord with many of us working guys.

The urge to change jobs can happen for many reasons, and at any age, but the motivation seems to hit hardest between the ages of thirty-two and forty-two. Is this "mid-life crisis," or just the "twilight zone" for men who are quietly experiencing the same frustration as Billy Crystal's character? Many describe feeling that life is slipping by—they want some joy in their work—and fearing they may miss the last good career opportunities to come their way. Some men are ready to jump to a new challenge, while others fear change.

What's Your Job Status?

Where do you stand with your career right now? Are you ready to take a leap? Taking stock of what you believe

about your own career is an important step before leaving
a position. I use a biblical metaphor involving the Israelites
to help individuals evaluate their true feelings about their
work situation. As you read the following, take a few minutes to determine if you are in *Egypt*, the *Desert*, or the
Promised Land in your current job.

Egypt

The Israelites were under oppression in Egypt. Conditions seemed intolerable and they wanted out at any cost.
As a people they were oppressed, angry, restless, and ready
for any means of escape. But God had a plan for their ex-
odus that would both bring glory to Him *and* allow His people to leave with dignity and with ample resources.

Andrew, a salesman, had made two impulsive job
changes. One was completely unsatisfactory and lasted
only nine months. His current job was not much better. He
had no plan, and had not prayed about the moves. His purpose in job-hopping was purely to escape—but he found
himself trapped in more inner conflict and unhappiness.
Now he was depressed—which is spiritual "Egypt."

When you are in a work situation in which you feel
trapped, while the life is being drained out of you, God *will*
reveal a plan for escape. It will require planning and being
ready to move when the time is right, though not necessarily on your timetable. Perhaps He will bring a great new job
your way, or maybe His plan is to give you strength to en-
dure the existing situation for a while longer. But you can
rest assured that He is preparing a way out for you.

The Desert

As Moses led the Israelites toward the Promised Land,
they followed a pillar of cloud through the desert by day
and a pillar of fire by night. As they wandered, God provided for them through an inexhaustible supply of clothes,

housing, and food in the form of manna. In this wilderness journey, God was building obedience and trust within His people. He wanted them to have faith in Him, even though they didn't know exactly where His plan would lead them. A. W. Tozer defines "faith" as looking to God as our one true source of direction and supply. When we are in desert situations, especially at work, it is critical that we turn ourselves fully to God, ready to grow in trust, ready to obey.

At times God may choose to provide you with a "desert" experience—that is, a job that's not bad enough to be "Egypt," or perfect enough to be the Promised Land. I call these "manna" jobs, because they meet basic needs. Check the following to see if you are in a "manna" job:

- The work is interesting but inspires no real passion. Assignments seem repetitious. ("Been there, done that.")
- You have identified your ideal job, but can't get there yet due to lack of education or experience.
- You envision a need for more money in the future (college for kids, retirement, etc.) but this job/career field can't provide it. (So this job will do—until something better comes along.)
- This job is providing needed experience and training for the ideal job.
- Though the work is uninspiring, you are earning good money at a time in your life when financial demands are high.

Prior to starting my current business I was in a "manna" job. The career consulting work was challenging but repetitious, and I was ready to move on. As I've said, my ideal was a part-time consulting position, combined with part-time ministry. I determined to use the last two years in this "manna" position to be productive for my employer—but also to gather industry information, save money for starting my own business, and pray for God's timing and direction.

What's the point here? If you take the wrong attitude, all you'll see is desert—a place of dryness and dead ends. You'll do a lot of whining. From God's perspective, the desert was a place of anticipation, provision, and preparation. God can use "manna" jobs to help us grow in obedience, to provide for our needs, to help us to pick up needed knowledge, or to get rid of negative habits that might inhibit future success. Have you ever been in a "manna" job—or are you in one now? If so, are you thankful? Do you make yourself miserable: complain, moan, and pout? Or do you drink or find other "escapes" to deaden the bitterness you feel inside? The only way to a Promised Land kind of job is the road that takes you through and *beyond* your own bad attitudes. Which is to say, the more you approach your life and work with a thankful, expectant attitude—willing to work and delay gratification—the more you will make yourself into the kind of man who *finds* Promised Land jobs.

Attitude is everything. So, as Philippians 4:6 says, "Be anxious for nothing, but in everything by prayer and supplication, with thanksgiving, let your requests be made known to God" (NKJV).

Here are some steps to take when you find yourself in "Egypt" or the "desert":

- Give thanks every day to God for His provision. Don't focus on what you *don't* have. Pray with your wife, pray with other men, and read God's Word.
- Ask God to reveal shortcomings in your life that need to be addressed before your next assignment. An honest relationship with other men can help. Seek to correct your shortcomings now.
- Be an excellent steward, and reflect God's love on your current job by the quality of your work, a positive atti-

tude, and by recognizing the value of present experiences that will assist you later.

- Begin a career search. Consult a career counselor, if necessary, and begin to design the ideal job for you.

Bill had labored in a high-paying union electrician's job for twenty years. Now he wanted out because the years of hard physical labor were taking a toll on his back. He was somewhere between "Egypt" and the "desert." His wife was concerned about his health and open to any change. Bill's objective was to start a small home business in computer supplies. He was fired up and ready to make this move when we talked—but it was also apparent that he was short on capital, needed some more computer expertise, and lacked bookkeeping skills. My counsel was: Stay another year on the job, save as much money as possible, and take some business and computer courses at the local community college.

Bill decided to listen, and by taking the time to prepare, he was able to launch his business successfully a year later. I appreciated his grateful spirit, his prayerful approach, and his discipline in preparing himself as he waited for the right timing and opportunity.

The Promised Land

Those of us who enjoy what we do, who experience passion and significance, have made it to the career "Promised Land." Does the Promised Land mean an absence of problems or frustrations? Of course not. But when you are there you will experience

- passion for your work;
- high energy to give to learning, achievement, and relationships;
- significance associated with the job;
- a sense of God's presence and being in His will.

Do You Know How and When to Leave a Job?

One of the first career counseling questions I ask a man is: "Are you running from your situation or going toward an opportunity?" Anyone contemplating a change should ask the following questions:

- Am I running from my situation?
- Am I too "frozen" to move?
- Am I going toward an opportunity?

Running From a Job or Career

Many men who leave a job for the wrong reason are running from a bad situation. If any of the three reasons listed below are your rationale for leaving a position, pray and seek counsel as to whether you need to stay long enough to work through your problem *before* you make a move. Trust me in this—the same problem *will* show up again, sooner or later, wherever you go!

1. Conflict. Sam complained to me, "The workplace is terrible, everyone has a bad attitude, the boss is a jerk, I have to challenge every decision, and everyone is lazy. I'm the only one working hard."

Sam may be right, but more often than not a dialogue like this indicates that Sam is part of the problem. He may be adding to conflict or even causing it because of a bad, superior attitude. Perhaps he has a "victim mentality" and sees everyone as "out to get him." He could also be covering up his poor performance or be short on needed social skills.

If you have regular conflict with others, sit down with a colleague, personnel manager, or career counselor and find out how you might be contributing to the problem. Take some tests and learn your behavioral style, so you know which traits push your hot buttons. Learn how to interact effectively with different people and their styles. (See chapter 5.)

On the other hand, some workplaces *are* full of people who are hostile. Conflict is constant, and you are not part of the problem. But, conflict is not an automatic sign that you should bail out. You can grow by learning how to deal with the situation, how to compromise, and how to work through the problems. Dealing with conflicts on the current job before leaving is a mature step, because difficult people exist in all settings.

2. Competence. Howard was a salesman who, unfortunately, had never mastered the art of sales. He was constantly changing jobs, hoping to "stick" somewhere. Many men run from a situation because they are not performing well in their present job. They may need more training, experience, or education. Many companies don't do a good job of training employees, but it is often difficult for us men to admit to our supervisors that we need help.

If you ever feel you need to leave a job and get a "fresh start," ask yourself if you're running from a setting because you feel less than competent. Before you leave take these steps:

- Assess your knowledge and skills. Do you need on-the-job training, more experience, education, or individual practice?
- Find someone in your field who can evaluate your skills, and then open your mind to the possibility of extra work to help you improve.
- Ask your immediate supervisor what skills need improvement, and get his or her advice about how to do it.

3. Confusion. I sometimes feel overwhelmed by the advancements in technology and the accelerated pace of life in general. How about you?

Many men I meet feel frustrated as the world accelerates and seems to pass them by. Sometimes they carry a sense of anger at an "unfair" situation. A move—any move—seems better than doing nothing.

But unless you've clearly defined your goals, it's usually best to stay where you are until you have developed a career plan. Again, changing jobs when you feel confused, bypassed, or resentful can result in transferring the same problems to the next assignment and going through the same repeatedly. Start a career-planning program that involves some training, if necessary, to keep up-to-speed with changes in your industry.

Being Frozen on the Job (Staying Too Long)

My career files abound with the cases of men who have stayed in a position longer than they should have. Some are ineffective, others are bored, and still others are frustrated with the level of challenge or responsibility. People stay too long for the following reasons:

1. *Comfortable.* Do you know anyone who is just "putting in their time and taking a check?" Eventually, the consequences could be termination, demotion, or living with a sour disposition. A move away from that so-called comfort zone can require a real jolt.

Recently, I received a call from the wife of a small-business owner. She said, "My husband has been a remodeling contractor for fourteen years. We don't have enough money, and our marriage is under great stress. He won't quit, and we're struggling every month. Is there a way you can help?"

When I got together with Fred, I learned he'd been fulfilling his dream of working for himself. But now his dream was dying, and he was resisting the idea of finding a new trade or a position working for someone else. He *needed* to move, but was afraid of the change because he thought he would lose his dream. One problem was that Fred's dream was too heavy on independence—and too light on balancing his supposed need to work for no one but himself with the fact that he was a family man with responsibilities. His adolescent drive for independence needed to mature into responsible, self-giving manhood.

If you are in a similar situation now, *set some clear financial goals.* If they are not met in your current work, *commit to finding a new job.*

Staying in a comfortable but unsatisfying job can involve a confidence issue as well. Many men aren't sure their skills are transferable, or that they can succeed in a new venture. John came seeking career help. "I've worked in the sawmill as a maintenance technician for fifteen years. I'm making way too much money to leave—but I can't stand the grease under my fingernails anymore!"

I've heard similar stories from attorneys, physicians, bankers, pilots, and pastors. If you ever come to this point in your career, it's time to trust God, pursue a new line of passion, and watch Him move wonderfully in your life. John sought counsel and then prepared to take a planned risk. He found a new career in an electronic business, starting at less money but with a brighter future. He and his wife prepared financially, then he took the step.

2. Avoiding Change. You may be a president, general manager, or department manager who no longer has the skill, knowledge, or desire to run a growing organization. You may have birthed and grown this "baby," and don't want to trust someone else to take over. At this point of transition, many organizations become stagnant and experience business reversals. If this describes your situation, you may need to step aside or leave the company completely. That's hard to take or even imagine, I know. Nonetheless, you may need to face this possibility.

Missionaries, pastors, and parachurch workers frequently call me with a different issue. They have lost their zeal for the work and secretly want to do something else, or their support is drying up. Many feel a sense of failure and that they are letting God down. They also have some fear of making it in the for-profit world. The bottom line is, they are avoiding change.

Bill and his family had an effective ministry overseas for eight years, supported by contributions. He told me he was angry because of the dwindling financial support. In his case, he thought he wanted to stay in the ministry. The obvious answer was for Bill to return to the U.S., get a job, and put the ministry on the back burner for a period of time while he sorted out the future. Although he resisted this option for a while, that's eventually what he did. It turned out to be an excellent choice for him, and he has remained in the business world performing lay ministry ever since.

Going to a Job or Career

When a man understands why he is making a career move and has sought God's direction, then he is generally making a move *to* a position as opposed to running *from* a bad situation.

The following are some good reasons for leaving a job:

- You feel it is time for a new challenge, or new responsibility. You've accomplished all you can in the current position.
- You need a lifestyle change: less hours, less travel, or less stress.
- There are illegal activities or ethical problems on the part of management or the industry.
- There are serious relationship problems that you have addressed to the best of your ability but which remain unresolved.
- You have a sense of God's call to a new position or to Christian service.

- The industry or the company is dying a slow death.
- The company is severely over- or under-employed.
- You need additional education or training that is not available on the current job.

Leave the Right Way

Leaving a job can and should be done in the best way possible, whether you are quitting for a better opportunity, resigning from an intolerable situation, or being fired or laid-off. As the door hits your backside on your way out, will former co-workers see a reflection of the kindness and patience of God, or a distraught, self-centered person leaving in bitterness? Yes, there are times when you may need to leave a job that is very bad indeed—where your pay is being withheld, you're being harassed or belittled or physically threatened or pushed to do something illegal. If so, I highly recommend that you report the situation to corporate heads, to government agencies—even to the law, if necessary. Conflicts of a serious, legal nature need to be handled through proper channels. Embroiling yourself in a battle or vendetta is a bad idea.

Under normal circumstances, though, here are some suggestions for leaving a position the right way:

- Finish with excellence any work to be done.
- Don't complain or cause problems before you leave.
- Seek to mend relationships that may have been damaged, as far as it is possible.
- Leave with humility, not a sense of arrogance.
- Leave quietly, thanking those who have helped you along the way (workers, vendors, customers, etc.).

Robert was the president of a manufacturing company subsidiary and suspected he was going to be terminated in two or three months. A major customer owed the company a long overdue $4 million. As we talked, he wondered if he should put most of his time into seeking a new position or vigorously pursuing the major account receivable before he left. His ultimate decision was to direct his energies primarily to his current company, and trust God to help him in his job search later. "It's the right thing to do," he said. He collected 90 percent of the funds, and within a few months found a new position managing a new facility in Asia.

Robert made a decision honoring God, and I believe God honored him in return.

Personally Speaking . . .

I served on the management team at a large Christian ministry—a "Promised Land" position, or so I thought. After an eventful three years of change and some turmoil, I knew the president wanted to demote or even fire me. (Look out "Egypt," here I come.) Seeing the handwriting on the wall, I chose to leave with dignity. In the month preceding my departure, I identified what factors I could control, and chose to take the following actions:

- I treated the president with respect, and prayed for him daily. This was not easy.
- I did my work with excellence, and left assignments in good order.
- I refused to complain, gossip, or bad-mouth the president to others.
- I arranged a meeting with the president to express appreciation for my time there and to discuss the timing and conditions of my leaving.
- I maintained positive contacts with people in the organization.
- I sought reconciliation with one of the vice-presidents with whom there had been great conflict.

Although my preference would have been to stay, I later

saw God's hand in the move in ways I could not appreciate at the time. I believe that God was honored, and my transition to a new career was smooth and free from personal bitterness.

No matter what part of the "job landscape" you are in—"Egypt," the "desert," or the "Promised Land"—*trust God*. If you seek His direction, you can always leave a position with order, dignity, and hope for the future—even in the worst situation.

God will direct our paths to exactly where He wants us, and there is a sense of peace that comes with knowing that our desire and His desire for us have come together in a unique way.

Changing careers or jobs is one of the most exciting journeys you will take in your life. Don't be intimidated by the challenges—do enjoy the adventure!

For Thought and Discussion

1. Where are you in your work right now—"Egypt," the "desert," or the "Promised Land"?
2. Have you stayed at a position too long? Is it time to change?
3. If you change jobs, would you be *going toward* an opportunity or *running from* a situation?
4. If you are in the "desert," are you prepared to focus on God, pray as if it all depends on Him, and work as if it all depends on you?

Conflict #4:
People Who Drive
You Crazy

Are you convinced that there are people God has put on this earth just to make your life miserable? How about

- the key customer who criticizes every sales move you make, and then tries to grind your margin down to almost nothing;
- the co-worker who for some reason doesn't like you or is out to "get" you;
- the clerk who takes forever to make those daily reports that you need to finish your work for the day;
- a manager who repeats directions over and over—and then looks over your shoulder until the job is done;
- the person who loves to socialize, when all you want is to be left alone so you can do your job;
- the loud, foul-mouthed person; or the hostile, complaining person; or the backstabber; or . . .

I have enough faith to believe that most people want to have congenial relationships. On the other hand, we've all met guys who go through life with a chip on their shoulder, creating conflict as they go. Working closely with others, we'll always find differences of opinion on minor issues (are the Bulls or the Sonics better?), or major issues (should we add a new product line and incur the additional expense?). Most of us have said at one time, "If it weren't for having to deal with *people*, this job would be perfect!"

In my experience, the majority of men who are fired are not let go because of technical problems or lack of knowledge but because they can't get along with one or more people in their work environment.

If you want to grow personally and professionally, you need to learn how to effectively manage conflict with others. In fact, I would say one of life's most critical skills is the ability to handle difficult interpersonal relationships.

Shoot-Out at the "OK Office"

For three years I managed a department in a large human resources division. Because of company growth, the function was split, and a woman named Linda was brought in to manage the other half of the department. As she moved in and carved out her "territory," things she said began to drift back to me in a roundabout way. She complained that "previous systems were poorly designed" and that "there are better ways to get the job done." She also told some untrue stories about our boss and mistakes he had made. Pretty soon nothing anyone else did was right.

Before long, I began to hate the smell of Linda's leather coat and perfume as she walked into the office every morning. I avoided her as much as possible and at times responded with short, cryptic, or sarcastic comments. At home, I vented my frustrations to Jeanne, criticizing Linda's lack of knowledge, her confrontive style, and her aggressive climb up the corporate ladder. The knot in my stomach grew bigger as the weeks went by.

Linda was a problem, true—but I did nothing to resolve the growing tension between us. That was because, up to that time, I had never learned to deal with conflict. She didn't like me, the feeling was mutual, and that was that. Looking back, I can see how I contributed to the problem, but at the time I felt like the innocent, aggrieved party. Although this was a difficult time in my life, I began to learn some things about myself and how to deal with conflict God's way.

Three Points of Conflict

There are many reasons why people don't get along in the workplace, but three key reasons stand out:

1. Something we value is threatened. If something that's important to you is in jeopardy, the natural reaction is to put up the defenses—maybe even pull out the big guns to strike back. What do you value that someone can threaten? Your reputation, integrity, competence, position, pay, peace of mind, or comfort zone? Linda threatened my reputation, chance for promotion, and the comfortable way I had always done things.

2. Poor communication. When problems develop between people, it's critical to keep the dialogue open. Instead, many of us choose fight or flight. The fighters keep the conflict going with retaliations, sarcasm, gossip, or shouting matches. That usually leads to one-way communication without much listening. My personal style leans toward flight—withholding needed information, cutting off most contact, becoming passive-aggressive. With poor communication, it is easy to misunderstand motives, misinterpret statements, and mistrust intentions.

3. Differing behavioral styles. People approach work and relationship differently. When we don't appreciate those differences, conflict is a natural outcome. People who naturally focus on tasks may seem insensitive to a man who is more people-oriented. People who are detail-oriented may seem small-minded and picky to a guy who naturally looks at the big picture. When you criticize someone who looks at the world differently than you do, the conflict begins and unity breaks down.

All three conflict factors were in place when I was hired by the general manager of a large pulp and paper mill. My mission was to mediate the differences between two technical managers that had severely hampered production. To get this conflict resolved, I locked all three of us into a hotel room, and we started working through the issues. Jamie and Red were technical managers whose functions required cooperation and support to meet daily production quotas. Both were committed to the company and wanted to do their jobs well.

Jamie valued organization and maintaining control, two elements that were threatened by Red's desire to take charge and create change. On the other hand, Red saw Jamie's conservative commitment to the *status quo* as threatening his bonus. They were at each others' throats constantly, arguing over scheduling and technical issues. Because they talked only when necessary, neither one understood the other's viewpoint and a gap in communications grew.

Jamie was detail-oriented, highly organized, and operated strictly on standard operating procedures—"the way it's always been done." Red liked to listen to the crew and change procedures when he saw a better way to get the job done. Jamie, the perfectionist, with strong tendencies to be introverted, said nothing and seethed inside when Red and his crew made one of their moves. Red looked at Jamie as an inflexible, "old school" technician who was behind the times. Being task- rather than people-oriented, he frequently said things to Jamie that were hurtful. Here we had a conflict in behavioral styles in how each guy approached his work—one flexible and creative, the other precise and structured.

Over a period of weeks these two learned to appreciate each other's style and began to communicate. Red and Jamie both said the key to their changed relationship was seeing the very different way they each approached their work. Now Red consults with Jamie before he makes changes, and Jamie admits that Red has some ideas he never would have thought of. Of course they still disagree at times, but they've built a solid working relationship by allowing their differences to complement each other instead of causing conflict.

Response to Conflict—God's Way and Man's Way

Conflict can be positive when honest differences of opinion lead to decisions to try new approaches or resolve problems. That is a win-win situation. But if issues don't get resolved and differences become personalized, the impact of conflict becomes negative. When we feel under attack by that person who seems to have it out for us, we can choose to respond in one of several ways:

- Retaliate or get even.
- Protect ourselves.
- Build the relationship.
- Confront the other person.
- Ignore the conflict.

Retaliation is the Clint Eastwood response, "Go ahead, make my day!" If this is your response to conflict, you may have a plaque on your wall that says, "I don't get mad, I get even."

No matter how good it might feel at the time, this response is never productive.

Self-protection is a natural human response to conflict, especially if something we value is threatened. No one enjoys conflict, but if we can't get beyond our first defensive reaction, we're stunting our personal and professional growth. When conflict comes in the form of criticism, you need to ask yourself, "Does this person have a point?" Or, "Is any part of what he said valid?" Then, "Is there an area to improve?"

We need to be open to criticism—accepting what is valid, and rejecting what is not.

Building a relationship is a powerful tool for resolving conflict. God honors peacemakers who promote unity and oppose dissension. If Red and Jamie had gotten to know each other as people, their differences would probably never have escalated to the point they did.

We can learn to see even the most difficult person, through God's eyes, as a unique creation. No one said it would be easy.

Confronting is sometimes the only way to resolve a conflict of ideas, attitudes, or actions. Of course, confronting is much easier when you have first built a relationship. This word has a negative connotation because too often confronting is done in anger. But anger does not have to be and, in fact, should not be part of the dialogue. Some issues need to be confronted head on, and there is nothing wrong with standing your ground in a strong manner.

Ignoring is appropriate in some cases. There are people who are socially inept, full of anger, or who think creating problems is a game. If you've tried building a relationship and tried confronting the problem, your last option is to *ignore* their actions—resisting the impulse to get even. Keep in mind the Proverb that says, "A gentle answer turns away wrath, but a harsh word stirs up anger" (15:1). Over time, even a person with this difficult profile may respond to your strong, patient manner, and begin to change.

Managing Conflict—a Look at Behavioral Styles

Research indicates that we respond in predictable patterns to situations we encounter—which shows our *behavioral style*. If you know your style and understand the traits of those around you, many conflicts can be avoided.

Gary was a machinist, and came to me because he was not getting along with his supervisor. When he received specifications for a new product, his boss would look over his shoulder "to make sure you get it right." Finally, in frustration, Gary asked his boss to leave him alone so he could get the job done. That caused a real problem. When I analyzed Gary's style, he saw that he was an independent, flexible guy who needed to work on his own. His boss was an extremely cautious perfectionist who had a need to control. They had a difference of style, which had escalated into a personal conflict.

Gary learned to respond to his boss with respect, and to explain why he worked more effectively alone. I suggested that Gary offer to review his work with his boss in steps, which addressed his boss's need for control. When Gary was able to see that his boss's hovering had not been an attack on his own competence, much of his anger dissipated. This allowed him to search for compromises that would address *both* their needs. In turn, as Gary was more open in sharing his work progress, the boss gradually felt less need to check up on him constantly.

The following is a list of behavioral traits that comprise personal style. There are no right or wrong styles, and everyone possesses some of every trait. But you will probably see that certain phrases describe you more than others.

Initiator
competitive; takes charge; persuasive; motivates; moves fast

Responder
reacts to, supports others; slower paced; calculates answers; conscientious; listens

Thinker
objective; measured; uses logic, thinks cause & effect; analyzes; factual problem-solving

Feeler
choices based on values; moves on intuition; promotes harmony, avoids conflict

People-Oriented
persuasive; personable; encourager; motivator; fun; creates change; optimistic

Task-Oriented
focuses on projects, results; end results count, not people; industrious

Structured
follows a plan; organized; needs closure; prefers policies, procedures

Flexible
freedom; adaptation; avoids deadlines, rules; changes decisions if needed

Introvert
quiet; calculated response; works from own thoughts; recharges by being alone

Extrovert
enjoys being around people; shares thoughts, feelings; outgoing; acts, then reflects

Concrete
takes in only necessary data; records what is seen, heard, or touched; factual

Abstract
ideas, concepts, feelings; takes in much data; emotional and intuitive

Sequential
moves in a step-by-step method; arranges thoughts logically; precision; orderly thought

Random
processes diverse, independent thoughts simultaneously; may appear disorganized

Go through this list and highlight the phrases that describe you. Now think of someone at work who is highly irritating to you. Which of these phrases seem to describe this person? If you find that the two of you have traits that are opposites, you've probably uncovered the biggest key to your conflict.

The truth is, every trait can be seen in a positive or negative light. For example, the structured person likes to be organized and follow a plan. But what if you see this person as "rigid and inflexible"? The people-oriented person is enthusiastic and optimistic. What if you see him as "unrealistic and impractical"? Some of us, by nature, see our own traits in the most positive light and others in the most negative. Others see the negative in themselves and the positive in others—but it's also a mistake. Either way, the root is self-centeredness.

Understanding your own style means not only learning what your strengths are but also how those "strengths" might be perceived by others. For example, I know that I make decisions based on feelings, I am slow to change, and random in my approach to tasks. The strengths I bring to situations are that I promote harmony, can work on a lot of things at one time, and don't jump to conclusions. I am also aware that others may perceive me as wishy-washy, disorganized, and too sensitive.

Here are two ways you can use your knowledge of behavioral styles to your advantage:

Adjust your style to prevent conflict. Once you have a basic understanding of your style and the styles of others, you can actually prevent conflict by deliberately adjusting your style in certain situations.

Mike is a people-oriented computer programmer, working in a world of people who are mostly task-oriented. Mike likes to get a lot of work done, but he also likes to take some time to get to know people on a personal level, ask about their families, and find out what makes them tick. When

Mike has a meeting scheduled with one of the men on his team, his natural style would be to spend the first ten minutes or so "shooting the breeze." But Mike has learned that this approach drives his co-workers crazy, because they're completely focused on the task at hand. Mike now gets right to the point in his meetings and uses coffee breaks or lunchtime for socializing.

Appreciate an opposite style. Kevin was a competitive, persuasive extrovert, who was always coming up with a new way to do things. He used to be completely frustrated by his boss who, Kevin felt, was always throwing cold water on his ideas. Once Kevin understood style differences, he began to see his boss in a new light. Instead of seeing his questions as an annoyance, he saw that his boss was bringing up things he had overlooked.

Men like Kevin, who make decisions quickly, can sometimes make errors of fact. His boss, who was slower to act, often pointed out problems that Kevin had missed. By allowing their different styles to complement each other, they became highly successful in being innovative without taking foolish risks. The boss appreciated Kevin for his originality, and Kevin appreciated his boss for his more analytical approach.

Do you think it's worth your time and effort to learn more about behavioral styles? One of the side benefits is that it can also help you be a more effective husband and father. Different styles exist within families too, and you might be surprised to discover that adjusting your style and appreciating differences can ease tensions at home. Testing is offered by career counselors as well as some community colleges. You can also get insight simply by reading books on this subject. Several are suggested in the Bibliography at the back of this book. Remember, the goal is to find positive ways to work effectively with all different kinds of people. You may not want to be best friends with everyone, but you'll be able to depersonalize conflict and ease much of the tension that comes from personality clashes.

Remember—the ability to get along with others can have a great influence on job promotions. It also pays personal dividends in peace of mind.

Responding to Conflict

Peanuts is still one of my favorite comic strips. Every fall, Charlie Brown is determined to run up and kick that football—and every year Lucy pulls the ball away at the last moment. Encountering conflict situations daily is about as certain as Lucy's actions.

Here are some ways you can respond to personal conflict:

When you might be the problem. When you have ongoing conflict, ask God in your prayer time whether you are the problem or at least a contributor to the problem. Ask Him to help you to identify the problem and find the solution.

With your prayer partner, wife, or close friend, discuss the nature of the conflict. Try to be objective. Don't be too quick to find someone who will agree with your side. Be open to honest feedback and options for handling an existing situation.

Examine your motives. Do you want to restore unity and harmony or do you really want justification for continuing the conflict? Are you looking for a way to prove yourself right?

Take restorative steps. If your actions have created a problem, go to that person and ask forgiveness. Be specific. "I've been disrespectful to you in the past and want to change that. Would you forgive me?" Not, "I'm sorry if you have taken offense at me."

Find a mentor or counselor to help you learn to handle

a situation better in the future.

Learn about your style to see what other styles have a tendency to rub you the wrong way, and vice-versa. Make it a point to adapt your style to others when it's needed— and appreciate those who are different from you.

When someone else is the problem. Remember that when you must *confront*, it is not to win your point or to make the other guy "see the light." It's an attempt to get to the facts, to resolve differences with the goal of *getting the job done.*

Ask for God's guidance in identifying the real problem and preparing the other person's heart. Ask Him to help you resolve beforehand any feelings of judgment, anger, fear, or superiority. Begin praying for those involved.

Evaluate the problem. Are there any other possible causes besides the present issues? Be open to hear facts that may not yet have come to light, which are causing the conflict.

Determine if you need to meet with the individual in person, or whether the situation can best be handled by ignoring the situation for the time being.

If *confronting* is appropriate, ask to meet with the other person at a mutually agreeable time. Sometimes when we get up the courage to meet, we want to "get it done right away," which does not always work.

State your reason for meeting and your desire to resolve the conflict. Listen to what they have to say, maybe take notes. If what they say gives you some new information, you may want to ask for time to think about the situation from this new perspective before you respond. If they say, "What conflict?" be prepared to give specific examples of what happened and how you felt.

Ask God to rebuild the relationship. Pray for the person regularly. Check your attitude and responses as you work together.

We are each designed uniquely, and we can choose to appreciate and honor our differences or allow them to irritate and annoy us. To those who have learned to manage conflict well, I say, make yourself available to others who need your maturity and experience.

Take a risk and learn how to manage those personality clashes. Be willing to look at yourself first to see if the problem is caused by the "speck" in your own eye. Step out of your comfort zone—both to look at yourself honestly, and to try to create peace with a kind of person you've never had to get along with before. It is possible that the person who irritates you most is a great complement to you?

Both you *and* your company can benefit if you learn to put aside your pride and begin to work together.

For Thought and Discussion

1. Is there someone you need to make peace with in the workplace?
2. Is the conflict a true difference of opinion or values—or is it a matter of style?
3. Do you know your style?
4. How could you adjust your style to avoid conflict?

Conflict #5:
A Terrible Boss

Bob came into my office with a woeful tale. As a middle manager in a family-owned business, he was consumed with anger, frustration, and anxiety. He reported to the owner who often screamed at his employees, including Bob. Even worse, the boss showed blatant favoritism toward his incompetent son. The owner also had a habit of making unscheduled inspections and criticizing what he saw without knowing the context of the activity. Bob had not received a performance evaluation or compliment in two years even though he had accomplished some great things.

I asked why he was still there. "The money is good, I like the work, the co-workers are great." His prayer and hope was that his boss would someday change.

When Your Boss Is Brutal

Bosses who are domineering, antisocial, and incompetent cause major turmoil in a man's life. Before I say anything, I want to tell you this: I believe that each manager, good or bad, has been allowed into our lives by our good and sovereign God for a purpose. If we place ourselves and our situation in God's hands, knowing He is the One who uses all things to train and guide us, then every manager will have a role in our vocational, personal, and spiritual development. One of our daily tasks as men is to ask God to help us see that purpose.

Let me ask you: What is your attitude toward authority?

More than a few manager-employee problems are the result of wrong attitudes. Life means having people in authority over us. Success or failure, peace or misery can come from learning how to cooperate with that authority— or continually bucking it. Many times problems with a boss are the result of how *we* act, respond, or communicate. Because of our inborn rebellious nature, men, we sometimes demand proof that someone "deserves" their position. But the Bible doesn't say that people are given authority because they deserve it. God grants this right to a specific person for a specific time and for a specific purpose. No matter how bad the circumstances seem, God will use that person in your life. As Christian workers, a careful and continual review of our attitudes will help us to line up with God's work in our lives.

What Is God's Purpose for Me in This Situation?

The following are some reasons why God may have allowed this particular boss in your life:

- as a challenge to mature you
- to help you learn to trust God
- to become a friend to this person
- to share Christ with him or her at an appropriate time
- to show others patience and discipline in the midst of trial, a witness to His grace and work in your life

- to teach you to confront with kindness
- to give you experience today that you will use later in life
- to prepare you for leaving at some point
- to help you understand and appreciate that God is in control
- to reveal your own areas for improvement
- to show you how to manage more effectively should you move into leadership

Carefully review the list and your history under managers or supervisors. Which of these purposes are being served now? Which were served by previous relationships with a difficult boss?

The Terrible Boss—Build Your Own

Counter to what you may think, bosses are people too. Some day you might be a manager and find yourself, in someone else's view, a terrible boss. When I present seminars, I generally ask, "How many of you have had a manager or supervisor that you would consider to be terrible?" Invariably, most hands go up. Are there any good bosses in the world? The definition of a terrible boss will be in the eye of the beholder. As an outplacement consultant, I have worked with numerous managers who have been fired for reasons including: ineffective interpersonal skills, theft, passive leadership, poor hygiene, incompetence, and insubordination. Talking later with their colleagues, some would be crying, naming virtue after virtue, while others would be lamenting the fact that management hadn't removed this guy long ago. Each of us will determine our criteria for a good boss and a lousy one, and these criteria will be different for different people.

Over the years, I've accumulated a list of traits that result in a boss being typed as ineffective, terrible, lousy, horrible—you get the picture. Take this opportunity to construct a composite of a terrible boss, using your experience. You may want to put a *checkmark* by those that drive you nuts and then prioritize the worst five:

Personal Traits

- all work, no fun, doesn't know when to laugh or play
- doesn't take work seriously enough
- moves fast and is only interested in results
- moves too slowly
- gives lots of compliments but seems insincere
- gets angry very easily; too harsh in his responses
- supercritical
- too touchy-feely
- views you as an object, not a person
- talks too much and doesn't get anything done
- takes credit for the work of others
- personal hygiene, dress, and work area are sloppy or inappropriate
- commits illegal acts, and asks others to do unethical acts
- talks behind the backs of employees

Competence Issues

- only communicates when you make mistakes; no compliments
- doesn't give enough feedback
- looks over your shoulder on every issue; micromanages
- is much too detail-oriented
- has no sense of detail; makes too many mistakes
- is too decisive and opinionated
- unable to make a decision, or stick with one
- doesn't delegate; keeps best assignments
- delegates, but then takes authority back

- avoids seeking your opinion and appears not to value your input
- doesn't give orders, directions, or goals, or does so poorly
- technically incompetent
- plays favorites
- does everything to look good for the next level of management
- commits acts of sexual or emotional harassment
- performance appraisals focus only on his/her interests, not your real performance
- does not represent your group adequately before management

Did you notice in this list that some of the "bad" traits are opposites? You may like a boss who is very hands-on and detail-oriented. Your co-worker at the desk next to you finds those traits annoying and suffocating.

It's important to acknowledge that there are work situations where the actions of the boss are potentially dangerous. He or she may exercise poor leadership in safety risk areas, or be emotionally unstable. Perhaps you work for a woman who is manipulative or enjoys "man-bashing," or for a man who ridicules and harasses women. Situations like these may require higher-level company intervention, law enforcement help, or legal assistance. If so, seek counsel from a friend, pastor, professional counselor, or attorney before you act.

Factors Contributing to a Poor Relationship With Your Boss

I've found it helpful to assist men in identifying the real cause of the conflict with their boss so they can create an appropriate action plan. Review the following to see if these apply in your situation.

Different styles. As we saw in chapter 5, behavioral style is a powerful influence on how we respond to situations.

I once worked for a manager whom I considered to be ineffective. But as I look back, it was not a good guy/bad guy thing, as I thought at the time. He was a quiet, task-oriented manager with a conservative bent who liked structure, order, and step-by-step transactions. I was an outgoing, people-oriented subordinate, had a desk stacked high with paper, and shot from the hip a lot. If I saw him as a terrible boss—I was probably his nightmare.

How has God designed you, and how has He designed your boss? You may have conflict with your boss simply because you see everything from a different perspective. You may need to plan ways around your differences.

Different values. In the workplace today, several generations may work side by side. Maybe you like to dress neatly but informally, while a suit and tie is the only acceptable office attire to your sixty-something boss. On a construction site recently, an older crew leader pointed to his young workers and said, "Look how sloppy they are." He was dressed in a knit shirt with a collar and neatly creased work pants. The crew wore jeans and T-shirts that didn't look all that bad to me. Were they sloppy, or was it a difference in perception?

Maybe your boss demands long hours, like he experienced "in the old days," while you place a high value on getting home to coach your kid's soccer game. Driven young managers may value challenge and confrontation, while you prefer more diplomacy and a less confrontational style.

As an individual, you have your own values, and often the roots of conflict spread in your relationship with your boss.

Lack of knowledge. I've seen managers who were promoted because they did their technical job well. But those who have not learned to manage effectively wind up causing frustration in the ranks. Lack of leadership may result in failure to represent the team or crew before higher levels of management for anything from needed equipment to pay increases.

On the other hand, some bosses are good managers but short on technical knowledge. This can put pressure on subordinates to do more work, and quickly creates resentment in the ranks.

Character traits. The manager who never gives praise, responds in anger, or uses bitter sarcasm will never win the hearts of his people. This type of communication has a chilling effect on relationships at work. Some bosses cheat, steal, lie, or take credit for your work. Working for a person like this leads to discouragement and to workers who can begin to doubt their own ability. If one area for the "bad boss" definition stands out, it is here.

For the Christian, this is a prime opportunity to do your work "as unto the Lord," and look to Him for the words, "Well done, good and faithful servant." It may also be a time to learn how to respectfully represent the need for change. Just remember not to *push* but to leave the outcome in God's hands.

Lack of commitment. Ron saw his banking career being put on hold. His boss of five years was looking toward retirement in two, and didn't want to rock the boat. Any changes or improvements Ron suggested always ended up on the manager's desk, and brought no action. Most people are committed to doing a good day's work for a good day's pay. If a manager doesn't really care about his work, being on different commitment levels will cause conflict.

Typical Responses Toward a Problem Boss

Being human, we will have natural emotional responses to a problem boss. But, we can—we must—manage these

emotions in appropriate ways. If negative emotions about
our manager color our working day, and then persist long
after we get home, there is a problem. Negative emotions
can include:

Anger. When the boss is inept, or mean, or doesn't seem
to care—and upper management has no clue—then frustration grows with every day. If a manager is putting people at
risk, physically or emotionally, anger may be an appropriate response. But left free-floating, anger affects the quality
of your work and your whole life. Anger also leads to complaining as you attempt to influence other people against
an unpopular boss. This is not healthy, or right, which is
why the Bible opposes it. Anger needs to be resolved before
it turns into bitterness, or into creeping dissension.

Anxiety. For a time I went to bed at night thinking of one
particular manager, and I'd wake up the next morning with
him on my mind. No surprise that small physical symptoms appeared. Ongoing anxiety can produce physical
problems—especially when things seem outside of our
control. Stress becomes *distress* as it builds and accumu-
lates. Accidents at work, lack of concentration, or health
problems will result when we don't deal with tense or un-
pleasant situations.

Revenge. Revenge is the decision to "get even" for real
or perceived slights. You may think, "I won't produce at a
level that will get him his bonus." Or, "I'll plant a few, well-
placed words with his boss, co-workers, and customers—
that will take care of him."

In the long run, revenge results in a rotten attitude—and
it destroys any positive influence we could have on the situation.

Here's my advice: *Don't do it.*

Pouting, martyrdom, or dropping out. George, a customer service manager, had been promised a support person, a raise, and a new computer. Now he had only broken

promises from the company, and he was feeling guilty about his pouting, passive/aggressive attitude. "I'm not going to do anything except the minimum. When my manager changes his attitude, I'll change mine."

In another situation, the martyr says, "If this is the way it is, I'll just live with it and suffer." Rather than dealing with the problem, a "poor me" attitude develops, neutralizing productivity—not to mention emotional and spiritual health.

Effectively Confronting

The above reactions don't solve problems or conflicts. You really have only three choices: resolve the situation, put up with it, or leave. The way out of a situation, more often than not, means confronting in a godly manner. Acting out of fear or anger is an ineffective way to live. In the chapter on lethargy, we discussed the difference between "goals" and "desires." We have to keep in mind what we can control (goals) and understand which results we would like to have but that we can't control (desires). We set action plans for goals, pray about desires, and always leave the outcome in God's hands, trusting that He will guide us on the job path of His choosing.

But when confrontation is necessary, the following are steps to take in a godly approach to speaking with a difficult boss:

Preparation
Pray daily for your boss. Your boss is loved by God, has redeeming qualities, and has value as a human being. Pray for the success of your boss and for spiritual awakening if he or she is not a believer. Pray that he or she will change in the way God wants, not necessarily the way you want.

Consider the fact that he or she is under pressure. These

pressures may come from numerous sources: upper management, the deadlines of work, family. There may be struggles you know nothing about. Pray for understanding and to let go of a critical attitude.

Give thanks to God daily for your work. It's possible to be thankful for your income—even as you plan your strategies for confrontation.

Pray for your attitude to be positive. Remember that the goal is to make a better work environment and get a job done better. Pray that God will help you see and accept specific technical, relational, or attitudinal problems that you may be contributing to the situation.

Read God's Word relating to relationship issues. I recommend reading Psalms, Ephesians, Philippians, and the gospel of John.

Confess your wrongdoing to God. If you have done things to provoke or put down your boss (complain, gossip, slow production), ask for forgiveness. And *stop.*

List specific negative acts, traits, situations, or omissions of your boss. What problems have involved you directly? What is the primary problem? Does the issue have to do with differing styles, credibility issues, differing values, the boss's lack of knowledge, or negative personality traits? Is this a situational issue, or has this been ongoing? You are not called to involve others unless you are a supervisor and the negative acts are directly impacting people for whom you are responsible.

Get a grip on your feelings. What is your primary response to the situation? Try to get beyond anger and see what the emotions are behind it. Are you frustrated? Do you feel unappreciated? Are you unsure of what your boss expects from you because directives are unclear, or change too often?

Identify the specific offense. Have feelings been crushed? Has there been lack of recognition or social graces toward you? Other possibilities are: verbal put-downs in front of others; interfering with work; illegal activities; undeserved criticism; sexual harassment; indecisiveness that has caused you to miss deadlines. Write them down.

Seek Counsel and Godly Advice.
   Select two or three people to review your situation. This may be another business professional, a pastor, a trusted friend, or your prayer partner. Choosing someone else in the same work environment can lead to complaining. At times a human resource professional can give advice. It may help to put your thoughts in writing to clarify them. *Note:* To you introverts who will only confide feelings to your trusty hunting dog, this is the time to step outside your comfort zone. Let someone come alongside and help you through the conflict.
   Invite an honest discussion—and be open to an evaluation of your role. Encourage questions about how you've responded and discuss times when you have done well and when you have done poorly. Ask questions such as, "Have I created some of the problem?" Or, "What aspects of the relationship might I have overlooked?"
   Ask one person to be your coach. Working through a situation with a boss can be more like a marathon than a sprint. Progress may occur over a period of time, and having someone to check in with is important. A part of my business is devoted to coaching individuals in this situation. Proverbs 11:14 (KJV) says, "in the multitude of counsellors there is safety."

Meet With Your Boss
   This can be a touchy situation, especially with a difficult boss, because you may not know what to expect. Before you enter this meeting it's important that you have dealt with your emotions. James 1:20 says, "For man's anger does

not bring about the righteous life that God desires." Fear and anger are two emotions that will make it difficult for you to carry out your mission successfully.

Remember that your goal is to find out what can be resolved, where you will need to "agree to disagree," and to honor the Lord. Go looking for information and a different perspective. Be prepared to discover things about your performance you didn't know and to receive offers of reconciliation. Also be prepared for increased hostility, coldness, or anger. Much will depend on the emotional state of the manager (which you cannot control) and your emotional state (which you can control).

Define in your own mind the reason for this meeting. Is this meeting a first-step fact-finding encounter? Do you want to let the boss know of your displeasure and get his or her reaction? Maybe it's a second or third meeting, and you've been unsatisfied with previous outcomes. Are you taking a specific problem and looking for a specific outcome?

Plan where this meeting will take place. With a purpose in mind, select a private setting where the boss can give full concentration. Pick a time that is least disruptive and decide if it should be at the office, over coffee, or out to lunch. On extremely serious matters, the professional atmosphere of the office is best.

Pray before entering the meeting. Ask God to direct the meeting and to control emotions as they arise. Ask God to reveal truth and to direct the meeting toward His solution. Ask for a humble and teachable spirit.

Have a verbal opening to start the meeting. Open up with respect and state your purpose. Even if your boss is unreasonable, his position commands your respect. Get to the point with a minimum of small talk and state the reason for meeting. For example: "Bill, thanks for the time today, I appreciate it. I really am enjoying the new production schedule, but I'm struggling with our relationship and some angry criticism I received about the scheduling process that I'm not sure is justified."

Express specific problems. "I want to discuss the number of times you've been angry with me in the last month. It's bothering me, and obviously something is bothering you. Specifically, last Thursday you read me the riot act when _____ happened. Can you help me? I want to meet your expectations. I acknowledge that my problem was _____. But I didn't think it justified your anger and criticism."

Define expectations with the boss. Review the boss's expectations for your performance. Ask what he or she wants from you in the way of responsibilities, reporting, or attitude: "Can we review your expectations for my position and talk about any areas that you feel need improvement?" Express your thoughts about how future exchanges might be handled: "Can we agree that if I've done something wrong, you'll pull me aside to discuss it?"

If there is a negative reply, or a non-response, you may have to decide if you want to become content in the situation, wait for your transfer (or his), or begin to seek a new position.

Determine the next steps, next meeting, or actions to be taken. After the meeting, bring closure by asking what the next action should be, or agreeing to meet at a certain time in the future. The boss may give you assignments, such as writing out your expectations, or setting new goals, which should be completed as quickly as possible.

What are the possible outcomes when confronting a difficult boss? Here are a few:

- You may lose favor and be pigeonholed in a job.
- You could be fired.
- You might end up enduring more overt or covert punishment.

- Things could stay the same.
- Conditions could actually improve!

The results may be positive, neutral, or negative. The important thing is that you have been respectful and have confronted the situation positively. Don't expect results right away, but continue to pray and work through the problem. At least you will know that you've achieved your goals and done what you could. You can now leave your desire for change in the hands of God.

It is clear that dealing with a difficult boss has a lot to do with our attitude. A boss who is making life miserable has only the control that you give him if you make the mistake of seeing him as more powerful than an all-knowing God. You must always be open to God's solution—which may include changing your boss or changing you.

As you work through each challenging situation, you will find yourself growing both in maturity and in your relationship with God as you seek to glorify Him.

For Thought and Discussion

1. Do you have a problem with your boss that needs to be resolved?
2. Have you identified the reason for the problem?
3. What steps do you need to take to confront this problem?

Conflict #6:
Breakdown in Integrity

Rod was the newly recruited president of an engineering firm. Shortly after taking over, he discovered code violations in a project that had been completed prior to his arrival. He brought the violations to the owner's attention and told him it would cost several thousand dollars to correct the error.

The owner told him, "Forget it, the customer will never know."

As I talked to Rod, I learned that several factors were weighing on him: He had a large house payment; his relocation to the area left him with few personal and professional contacts; his "bird in the hand" was a six-figure salary and a great future in a growing company. The original problem was not his doing, but his strong principles were causing him distress. Rod was faced with a major decision—to go along with the boss, or stand for what he knew was right.

Rod decided to push for correcting the design flaw. But in subsequent discussions, the owner refused to consider any of the solutions Rod proposed. He ultimately resigned and left the company without a job in hand.

What do Rod's actions demonstrate to you? What would you do in such a situation?

What Is Integrity?

I never tire of hearing the story of Eric Liddell, a Christian from England who chose to withdraw from the 100-meter dash in the 1924 Olympics because the race was to be held on a Sunday. Here is a man who acted in accord with his beliefs. Are you a man of integrity?

Our immediate response *wants* to be *yes*, because the majority of us want to be seen as having integrity. But job conflict results as a man faces choices about actions and decisions that challenge his belief in himself—when something he is being asked to *do* doesn't line up with who he believes himself to *be*.

Simply stated, integrity is *acting consistently in accordance with a set of beliefs*. Men of integrity will consistently demonstrate these qualities in their thoughts, words, and actions:

Character: higher qualities, good traits by nature

Decency: dignity, respectability

Honor: respect, reverence

Principle: law, regulation, self-rule or control

A recent magazine article described two types of integrity: *conditional* and *intentional*.

Conditional integrity says, "I'll do the right thing as long as it doesn't cost me deals, dollars, or difficulties." *Intentional integrity* means doing the right thing regardless of the cost. Rod certainly demonstrated intentional integrity in his decision.

By What Standard?
     Integrity begins with defining your standards. For those of us who have decided to follow Christ, the Bible is the basis for principles that will guide our actions. The man with integrity has pure motives and is not looking to better himself at the expense of others, to manipulate situations to his advantage, or to take something he doesn't deserve.
     When faced with ethical decisions, a man of integrity will always ask, "What's the right thing to do?" and then refer to the body of principles that guide his life. If he only asks the question, "What are the possible consequences of performing this act?" he is practicing conditional integrity. Rotary International, a premier business association, has a "Four-Way Test" for its members:

- Is it the TRUTH?
- Is it FAIR to all concerned?
- Will it build GOOD WILL and BETTER FRIENDSHIPS?
- Will it be BENEFICIAL to all concerned?

     Sounds biblical, doesn't it? Conflict begins when we make decisions that don't line up with our belief structure.
     In the marketplace, you'll be challenged with both large and small issues that will eventually determine your character. Your faithfulness in the small things will often determine how you face larger issues. Here are some traits of a man with integrity:

- He does what he says he will do.
- He does not lie to cover indiscretions.
- He is vulnerable and can admit when he is wrong.
- He is consistent in performance, temperament, and relationships.
- He treats others with love, dignity, and respect.
- He makes decisions based on ethical principles, not on how he is affected personally.

- He follows the intent *and* the letter of a policy, procedure, or law.
- He gives credit where credit is due.
- He does not cheat, steal, or deceive.

Why Is Integrity Such an Important Issue Today?

The working world is fast-paced and increasing in intensity every year. Pressure is on the president, sales manager, production worker, and warehouseman to get more done with fewer resources. In some cases men work hard at a wage that doesn't seem fair, while the top management guys are making a bundle. It can be tempting to take an illegal shortcut, tell a lie to cover a mistake, or blame someone else for a delay. It's tempting to do *whatever* is necessary to get the job done.

Leo had an excellent law practice with a large firm, but the pressure was mounting for more billable hours per month. Here's the dilemma he presented to me: "I can charge large clients five or six extra hours a month for research to protect them in case of a problem. I could sure use the extra hours to meet my goals. Even though this is legal, as a Christian I can't justify it." Leo eventually left the practice rather than compromise his principles.

With the influence of today's self-centered world, conditional integrity can become a habit. The standard for "honesty" today is *expediency*—say whatever works—instead of factual truth. When we are faced with issues of integrity, we can have conflict over what our response should be.

You and I face decisions every day that challenge our commitment to intentional integrity, some small and others major. Below are some examples of common situations that you may face at work:

- Making a co-worker look bad in front of the boss in order to deflect attention from your own shortcomings.
- Withholding information from a manager or co-worker to make a point, to get even, or to make your efforts look better.
- Telling a "little white lie" to cover a small mistake, or a "whopper" to cover a major blunder.
- Invoicing a customer for hours you didn't work, or doing work the customer does not really need. This is a big challenge for everyone from CPAs and attorneys to automobile mechanics and other repair services.
- Not correcting errors made in your favor by customers or vendors—for example, when a bill is overpaid.
- Taking credit for something that someone else has done.
- Deceiving a customer by providing less service or product than he paid for.
- Not paying a full commission or bonus to an employee or a partner or who has earned it.
- "Cooking" the financial books before the IRS, state auditor, or potential buyer inspects them.
- Taking supplies (pencils, paper, tools) or using company equipment (long-distance services, copier, postage meter).

Why People Fail to Act With Integrity

There are several reasons why maintaining integrity can be difficult:

Lack of conviction. Some men have not defined the set of principles they believe in. They may not know what God has already told us in the Bible about His established principles. Perhaps they did not see principles modeled as they were growing up.

Failure to trust God. Sometimes even honorable deci-

sions can result in negative consequences. Failure to trust
God in these circumstances can lead to compromising values.

Greed or envy. When we want more than we have, or
want what someone else has, then greed and envy become
negative motivations. One example is cheating on business
or personal taxes. Often the rationale is that taxes are too
high, or that "everyone else does it." It can also cause us to
put someone else down to make ourselves look better.

Self-protection. Fear of failure, or of looking bad to others, are other reasons we fail to act with integrity. I've
worked with men who have been fired for lying just because they didn't want to own up to a problem they'd
caused.

Build Credibility Through Honesty and Openness

We build credibility by acting out our beliefs in a consistent manner over time. As a guy who wants to be honest,
I've never discovered why it's so hard to admit when I have
made an error. I have covered up, told "little white lies,"
and given terrible excuses. No one likes to fail, but when
you do, here are some appropriate responses:

- "I didn't do what was expected. I apologize and I won't
  let it happen again."
- "I underestimated the time and resources necessary to
  make the project successful."
- "I lost the tool. I had it yesterday, and I can't find it today."
- "It was my responsibility. I need to investigate more to
  determine why this didn't work."
- "I'm sorry I didn't call. I forgot, and that's not acceptable. Please accept my apology."

- "I promised to cover and didn't. There is no excuse" (even if there was a plausible explanation).
- "I failed to maintain the preventative maintenance schedule on the machine. I know the importance of doing so now."
- "Fred is taking the heat for not getting that report in on time. I failed to get my support documentation to Fred on schedule, so I contributed to the problem."

Benefits of Acting With Integrity

A man reaps what he sows. "Do not be deceived, God is not mocked; for whatever a man sows, that he will also reap. . . . Let us not grow weary while doing good, for in due season we will reap if we do not lose heart" (Galatians 6:7, 9, NKJV). If our goal is to be men of integrity, we cannot live dishonestly, use excuses, or be rebellious.

The benefits of being known as having integrity are:

Trust and respect. People will trust us as we act with principle, dignity, and honor. This leads to being respected in your work environment.

Responsibility. In time, a person who acts with integrity will be a candidate for more responsibility. Ethical leaders want to be able to delegate to those who will support the vision and mission of the company. They want men who will protect company resources, whether intellectual properties or tools.

A strong relationship with God. The Christian man of integrity is seeking to honor God. God responds by supporting us with "His right hand." The Psalmist writes, "Who may stand in his holy place? He who has clean hands and a pure heart, who does not lift up his soul to an idol or swear by what is false. He will receive blessing from the Lord and vindication from God his Savior" (Psalm 24:3–5).

No one is perfect. We all makes mistakes, but thankfully

God's plan includes grace that covers our sin as we seek to be conformed to His image.

Peace of mind and self-respect. Knowing that you have nothing to hide relieves the pressure of trying to cover things up. There may be nothing worse than living with a guilty conscience that results from actions that don't line up with your stated principles.

I wish I could tell you that if you act with intentional integrity, nothing bad will ever happen. Unfortunately, this is not the case. Rod's decision not to compromise his integrity cost him his job.

In certain work environments, the man who stands firm may be pressured to go along with the group. Peer pressure can be severe when you refuse to

- pad the service repair bill;
- cover for a mistake someone else has made;
- stretch your coffee break past the time allowed;
- look the other way when supplies are stolen;
- sabotage an unpopular boss;
- cheat on your time card.

No one wants to feel like an outcast. In situations like these, your ability to trust God will be tested.

My recommendation for dealing with a breach of personal integrity is this:

- Admit the problem, and list examples of when you have compromised your principles.
- Revisit the principles that you desire to live by and evaluate those you have violated. Write out where you have failed.
- Confess your sin to God and ask forgiveness.
- Ask forgiveness of others, or make restitution if your action has emotionally, physically, or financially hurt someone.

- Seek out a counselor or prayer partner to help you get through the current situation and to break any bad habits. Make yourself accountable while you are establishing new habit patterns. Be prepared to discuss any relapses with him.

The immediate discomfort of getting through the problem is usually far less painful than laying awake at night with a guilty conscience.

Confronting Others Who Have an Integrity Problem

Jim, a worker with a house-cleaning company, sees his partner take a candy bar from a kitchen cabinet. What should he do? Confront him? Tell the boss? Say nothing? What would Jim's motive be in saying something, or in reporting the action?

I believe we have a responsibility to confront another person who is compromising their integrity when we work closely with them. I don't want my integrity called into question by illegal or immoral activities occurring in my presence. With another Christian we can use biblical standards. With others, principles about truth, social standards, and obeying the law will often suffice to make your point. A "holier than thou" sermon will not be received well and will miss the point.

Here are some steps to take when you catch a co-worker in a wrongful or illegal act:

- Explain why you believe their actions violate a law, rule, or policy of the company. Describe the facts as you see them.
- Confront with love, dignity, and respect. Be humble and nonjudgmental. Offer to help in any way possible.

- Assist the individual in developing options to resolve the situation. Be a sounding board and coach.
- Pray for the individual prior to your first meeting, during your contact, and thereafter.
- Seek God's direction to decide if the infraction is serious enough to be reported or whether you should handle the situation yourself.

When Called Upon to Compromise Your Integrity

Hank, a customer service professional in the electronics business, found himself in a compromising situation. His manager asked him to obtain information by calling competitors and posing as a potential customer. Hank experienced inner turmoil for a couple of days before he went back to his boss. In responding to the situation, he took the following steps, which offers a good model for any of us:

- He prayed for God's guidance, that the manager would be prepared for the meeting, and that a solution would be found.
- Hank explained to his boss why the proposed action violated his principles. "I have made a point not to deceive people as a matter of principle. I wouldn't do it to you or my company, and to do so even with a competitor goes against what I believe."
- He attempted to clearly understand his manager's point of view. "Tell me why you think this request is legitimate and what we hope to do with the information."
- He offered alternative solutions for accomplishing the task. This required looking for innovative approaches. "I believe I could get this information by just telling them what I'm doing and why. I also believe data may

be available in the library and through public records of previous bid contracts."

• If ordered to proceed, Hank was willing to take the consequences—to quit, be demoted, or fired.

In this case, Hank's boss was willing to accept the alternatives he presented. In resolving conflicts of integrity, creative alternatives are often the key to a happy ending.

How important is your character? This question begs for an answer as we are bombarded daily with opportunities for compromise. Understanding what we believe and establishing accountability with other men will remove much of the conflict in our quest for integrity. Developing character requires following God and seeking to live a life holy and set apart. As imperfect human beings, we have God's grace and forgiveness.

Thank God, we go forward every day with the opportunity to be men of integrity.

For Thought and Discussion

1. Are there any current situations where you are acting against standards you know to be right? What is the situation?
2. Can you think of situations in the past when you have acted with *conditional* rather than *intentional integrity*?
3. Can you think of situations in the past when you have acted with *intentional integrity*? What was the outcome?
4. Is there anyone you know who is acting outside the boundaries of integrity? What is the situation? Do you have any responsibility to intervene?

Conflict #7:
Sexual Attraction

Robert was tired after his cross-country flight the night before with his consulting partner. He was working with a Fortune 100 company and planned to meet with ten area managers to introduce operational changes. Two of the managers were very attractive women. Robert ended up with Brenda in his small discussion group. All day it seemed they just happened to sit next to each other. They talked business and joked. At the end of the day, two-person teams were given an assignment to be completed that evening. Robert was paired with Brenda.

When discussing where to meet, Brenda suggested, "How about your room at 7:00?" Robert's immediate reaction was—"Sure, see you at 7:00." He didn't think much about it until 5:45. Then some questions began to drift to the surface of his mind. Was it appropriate to meet this woman alone in his room?

What's wrong with this picture? Or was there anything wrong? Could this have been a harmless meeting—or was it an open door for the start of something bigger? As you read the story, how did you react to Robert's situation? Go ahead with the meeting? Call and cancel? Reschedule for Brenda's room? Find a neutral location?

A Line in the Sand

Alex is attracted to his married secretary. She's beautiful, competent, and seems somehow lonely and vulnerable. Recently, he's found himself touching her on the shoulder, calling her to his desk more often, and brushing against her as they sit and talk. This guy is playing with fire.

As long as men and women work in close proximity, the emotional and physical attraction can heat up fast. If you have any blood pumping in your veins, you'll experience an immediate reaction to certain women. But as men committed to honoring God, there is a line we need to draw between *reaction* and *pursuit* when it comes to female co-workers.

Yes—There Are Right and Wrong Relationships

It's easy to define off-limits:

- For a married man—any woman other than his wife.
- For a single man—any married or engaged woman.

A man should always take the lead in directing a relationship. He knows when he's beginning to look longer and think more than he should about an off-limits woman. He knows when she's flirting with him.

Jerry was a successful salesman, married, the father of two children, and active in numerous programs at church. Cheryl was his sales support person in a fast-growing electronics company. Jerry wasn't sure why, but he asked

Cheryl to lunch to discuss a strategy for dealing with two key customers. The lunch went for two hours with work issues taking maybe half that time. She talked about her goals and desire to move up in the company. He discussed his family and a problem he was having with his wife. Cheryl was understanding and showed compassion, which was a real encouragement to Jerry. The next day they had coffee . . . the pursuit was on.

By the time we talked, Jerry's affair with Cheryl had cost him his marriage. Now remorseful, he still wonders how the relationship progressed to the point it did and what he should have done differently at the beginning.

The term *pursue* means "following with a view to over-take—to chase after." It's an overt act that requires some planning. For men, the pursuit process may appear inno-cent at the start. A relationship begins based on "deeper" communications—you've found a soul mate, someone who understands you. But inevitably the intensity increases. A kiss in the elevator or the parking garage, and finally an eve-ning or weekend of physical intimacy . . . after which most guys say, "I never intended to let it get this far."

The Eight Steps of Pursuit

When a man begins to cross that line with a woman at work, he usually follows a predictable pattern:

1. *An initial look and "reaction."* For some reason, Mary Beth has a certain attraction when she enters your de-partment. Maybe it's her hair, her laugh, or the way she looks you in the eyes. It's not unnatural to notice a "Mary Beth," and our tendency to react will probably be with us the rest of our lives.

No harm, no foul as long as we stop there.

2. *The second look.* You find yourself . . . looking again, and again . . . anticipating her appearances in your office.

If these reactions are occurring, it's probably because you're thinking about her too much. You're crossing the line between reaction and pursuit. *Here is where you need to stop.* Recognize the danger. Take steps to eliminate or minimize your contact. Discipline your thought life.

3. Thoughts. The next step in the escalation process is thinking about different ways to "get to know her better." You may make note of her schedule and arrange yours to see her more often. Perhaps you call her to discuss an issue that could easily be handled by someone else. At some point you may begin fantasizing about her in a romantic situation. You find yourself thinking about her more often—on breaks, during your daily commute. You may even feel energized. At this point, you may begin to rationalize that she is "good for you."

4. Rationalization—Part 1. In order to ignore inner warnings, rationalization begins in earnest. "Nothing will come of all of this." "I just need someone to talk to." Or, "My wife is busy with—housework, the baby—and besides, she can't really understand the situation at work anyway." Then, "She's just a great friend."

Maybe you have already committed adultery in your heart. It is still not too late to escape relatively unscathed, although you may need to take more drastic steps: Request a transfer to another department, or even look for another job. If you are married, you certainly need to examine your marriage and seek counsel if your relationship with your wife is strained or in trouble.

5. Action. When the opportunity is right, you are already prepared for action. The words appear without any conscious effort—an invitation to coffee, or lunch, or dinner. You've established a comfort level and are building up trust. You begin to spend more time together . . . when "suddenly" one night or one afternoon you find yourself caught up in physical intimacy.

6. *Cover-up.* One evening your wife innocently asks, "How are things at work? Who you do you have lunch with these days?" The thought kicks in, "Does she know about. . . ?" Then out of your mouth comes this response, "Oh, just the same old guys. We play a little basketball." Or, "I've been so busy I don't have time for lunch." This cover-up can occur at any of the stages described above. And it's one of the big "red flags" that says you have crossed the line. If you ever find yourself being less than honest with your wife, this may be one of the last warning signs God gives you.

7. *Rationalization—Part 2.* I have heard the following words in one form or another numerous times: "My relationship at home is not that good. And while, as a Christian, I will stay in the marriage, I need to have someone who respects me. God has sent me Jane for that very reason." Or, "It can't be that bad. I have someone to talk with when I don't seem to be able to communicate with my wife." Then, "This will make me a better husband and father." Or, "My wife and I haven't had sex for three years, and at least there's an emotional connection here that gives me hope." And on . . . and on . . . and on.

8. *Hardening of the heart.* At this point you are in a full-blown affair, or have built a strong emotional relationship and have decided to end your marriage. "I think that I married the wrong person in the first place. It was a mistake, and God would rather have us both be happy than be together in a terrible marriage." Or, "My wife is cold and has emotionally abandoned me—that's grounds for divorce." Then, "My wife will be much happier without me around, and God will protect the children." Or, "God doesn't like divorce—but it's not the unforgivable sin, and He'll forgive me." I have heard single Christian men say, "She isn't happy in her marriage, and her husband is a jerk. She deserves better." Needless to say, God's Word is clear on the

issue: There is no excuse for the sin of adultery.

The good news is God always provides a way back, even from this phase of the pursuit process. But the further you go, the more difficult and damaging it becomes.

Not-So-Obvious Pursuits

Pursuit may not always result in sexual encounters, but it can lead to an emotional affair. Emotional affairs suck the energy and passion from your marriage even if there is no physical component. The following are some signs of a not-so-obvious involvement:

- invitations to a non-work event (coffee, lunch, volunteer group meeting)
- touching on the arm, shoulder, or hair that is not accidental
- a show of vulnerability on the man's part (discussing a problem at work, at home)
- an expression of flirtation—joking around, extra looks, saying nice but silly things
- extended looks in the eyes during a normal conversation
- compliments about personal issues (her clothes, hair, perfume, etc.)
- an extended time of listening to her personal problems, asking probing questions, siding with her against her boss or her husband
- "innocent" touching—like squeezing her arm or a back rub in the office

All of these actions can be innocent if they occur infrequently and not always with the same woman. It's when they increase in frequency and are usually with the same woman that the innocence is gone.

Be honest, men—some of us crave the emotional excitement this type of flirtation generates. We want to see how close we can come to the chasm without falling in. But as men of integrity, the idea is to see how far *away* we can stay from sin.

For those who choose to follow God, there will be many checks and balances along the way:

- Your conscience will be active—sometimes whispering, sometimes yelling.
- Your prayer or time of worship will become dry—or you may avoid it.
- You may become irritable and grouchy—especially with your family or Christian friends. (Guilt does that!)
- You may become depressed, have trouble sleeping, lose or gain weight.

Leaving the Pursuit

Leaving the pursuit is really not that difficult if you are committed to doing so. Getting rid of a negative, sinful habit pattern is the first step in restoring relationships at home. The consequences that result from wrong actions eventually will be played out. To turn the situation around follow this exit strategy:

- Quit deceiving yourself.
- Confess your thoughts and sin to the Lord in prayer. Ask for direction and forgiveness, and begin to glorify God in word and action.
- If the attraction process is in the early stage, just stop the pursuit and cut the cute stuff.
- If you've moved to advanced stages, have a direct meeting with the woman and ask her forgiveness. Take responsibility for the relationship—and for ending it.
- Immediately return to a professional relationship, which is focused on work.

- If you've crossed the line to adultery, request a transfer to another position, or resign. (Sometimes we have to take the tough consequences.)
- If the attraction remains strong, talk to your pastor and seek a regular prayer time with him or another trusted brother in the Lord. You may need to see a professional counselor.
- Tell your wife what has transpired when you believe it can serve a good purpose. Telling her in order to make you feel better and to relieve personal guilt is not a godly purpose.
- Find a Christian man who will hold you accountable. In my experience, most men who fall sexually do not have accountability in their lives.

Many of the women I work with are professional, intelligent, and physically attractive. Much of my work involves one-on-one meetings and the discussion of personal issues. I have a mechanism that I use to keep my professional relationships professional:

- I pray every morning asking for God's protection.
- I ask myself if my actions will lead them closer to an initial relationship with God or additional knowledge of God.
- When my thoughts wander, I move immediately in my mind to Jesus Christ, the One who died for me—it always brings me back to solid ground.
- I always try to meet with women in public places, or in my office with the door open.

At a luncheon I was talking with a man who'd been a Christian a long time. He said, "I don't have trouble with that sexual temptation stuff. I'm way beyond that in my life." *Red flag!*

Peter told the Lord, "I will never disown you" (Matthew

26:35)—and within twenty-four hours he'd rejected Christ three times (Matthew 26:69–74). Any man who thinks he has arrived at a point where he can't be tempted by sexual chemistry is deceived. Scripture says, "So, if you think you are standing firm, be careful that you don't fall" (1 Corinthians 10:12).

Women in the workplace often give respect to those in power, or to those who are kind and accommodating. Their attention fulfills a basic need men have to be respected. Pride races in when a man thinks, "Hey, she's right! I do make a difference in this department—I'm pretty great." Flattering comments from an admiring co-worker can jump-start the "pursuit" process.

A Breath of Fresh Air

When a Christian man really lives his faith in the workplace he will stand out. Many women are lonely, starved for affection and needing attention, appreciation, and approval. The man in the workplace who exhibits godly qualities may draw the attention of these women. Even if your intentions are honorable, it is possible for a woman to become infatuated with you. You will always need to be alert for any signs that this is occurring, and not allow yourself to be drawn in by someone else's need.

As you operate with God's confidence at work, you can go home to your wife and family in peace, not with guilt or shame based on a wrong relationship at work.

As Paul Harvey would say, "Now for the rest of the story." This chapter opened with an account of Robert mulling over a decision. Should he meet with Brenda in his hotel room? Let's take a look at the situation again.

First of all, there were signs throughout the day that Robert was paying more attention to Brenda than may have been healthy. He insisted his intentions were innocent—but when he got honest, he had to admit he sent out "signals" that he was enjoying the growing sense of intimacy.

Robert chose not to meet with her alone. He rescheduled the meeting, and then made it as brief as possible.

He chose right.

Trusting God in the area of work relationships with the opposite sex is a challenge. *Who are we going to serve?*

For Thought and Discussion

1. Am I in pursuit of a woman at work (or elsewhere)?
2. Am I treating this woman the way I want other men to treat my wife or daughter?
3. Do I ever say things (even as a joke) that could be misinterpreted by a woman in my work environment?
4. If I am known as a Christian, is Christ being glorified in all my relationships?
5. Am I avoiding even the appearance of evil?
6. Do I have another man (or men) to hold me accountable?

Conflict #8:
Offensive Language

People judge your *character* and *abilities*, in part, by how you communicate. How you are perceived can impact promotions and work relationships, as well as your testimony for Jesus Christ. Whether he is a Christian or not, I encourage every man to clean up his language and to use words that encourage those around him.

Three areas in which the tongue causes conflict on the job are *criticism, gossip,* and *profanity.*

Maybe you work in an atmosphere where criticism, gossip, and crude language are the norm. Maybe your own tongue is out of control. It's easy to find yourself picking up the expressions of the guys around you. Sometimes an off-color joke is even funny—should we laugh? Are there times when we need to be "one of the guys"? Is it possible to let someone know we're offended without offending that person in return?

Power of the Tongue

The book of Proverbs speaks a lot about use of the tongue. When a man uses positive words he will

- nourish and encourage others (10:21);
- keep himself from trouble (21:23);
- be satisfied (18:20);
- be wise and discerning (17:28);
- be valued by leaders (16:13);
- find joy (15:23);
- know the right thing to do (10:32);
- have great power (25:15).

These benefits encourage me to choose my words wisely. Words aptly spoken have the power to educate, encourage, equip, energize, and evangelize those in our network of contacts. Even words of discipline and correction—voiced with gentleness and care—have this same power.

One of my favorite pastors, Tom Howard, says that we can be either a thermostat or a thermometer. The thermometer only *reflects* the environment. But as thermostats in our work environment, we can help to *set* the temperature. We can bring a positive influence even when those around us are negative.

Those who use words foolishly are likely to experience the negative consequences described in these verses from Proverbs:

- Sin will occur with too many words (10:19).
- With his mouth the godless destroys (11:9).
- A gossip betrays confidence (11:13).
- He who speaks rashly will come to ruin (13:3).
- A deceitful tongue crushes the spirit (15:4).
- A gossip separates close friends (16:28).
- He whose tongue is deceitful falls into trouble (17:20).

If you are experiencing problems at work because of someone's mouth—yours or anyone else's—you need to address the matter directly. Perhaps you need to learn self-

control. Maybe your co-workers or managers provide a stream of criticism, gossip, or profanity. A big part of your conflict may be, "How do I model a different approach without being a holier than thou, Bible-thumping, self-righteous Christian?"
Here are some solutions.

Criticism

Criticism is fault-finding, disapproval, accusation, or rebuke from one person to another. People who are critical often have learned this behavior in their family of origin. They may also have personal insecurities, prejudice, a need to be in control, or fear of failure.

Two key elements of criticism are judgment and sarcasm.

The judgmental or critical personality. Nelson, a production line supervisor, had an I-am-better-than-you attitude. His words were not aimed at helping. His goal was to point out a weakness and make himself look better in the process. If a worker did ten things right and one thing wrong, which one did he notice? His radar seemed to be tuned to catch the slightest mistake.

The judgmental person will try to keep other people in place by pronouncing a "sentence" of inadequacy. "You haven't learned to use the computer in six months, and you'll never get it." Or, "You have to work harder. You always do the wrong thing." Or, "You'll never get this problem solved." Or, "Can't you do anything right?"

The key difference between "evaluating" and "judging" is *attitude*. Are the words intended to help a person rise to a higher level of performance, or only to point out flaws? Many people don't know how to help in a positive sense, so they criticize. A critical spirit casts a shadow over the work environment and stifles creativity. Men living in a godly manner lift up, heal, and encourage—rather than putting down, hurting, and discouraging.

Sarcasm

Sarcasm can come as a response to a situation we don't like but don't want to address directly. Taunts and expressions of contempt are usually an attempt to be funny at another's expense. A sarcastic comment can make a point, but it always tears down someone or something in the process. There is no positive purpose for sarcasm.

I once was master of the one-line quip and put-down, something I have made a great effort to correct. One of my colleagues was extremely detail-oriented, slow to act, and was late with a major report. I merely said, "Will we have the report before the Second Coming?" That question might have been funny . . . if I'd been joking. But said in a sarcastic tone, it had a barb and definitely closed communication between us. The difference between humor and sarcasm is often in the tone of voice and body language.

Complaining and Gossip

"It's 9:45. Let's go!" At the insurance company, the guys go down to the cafeteria for a latté and a bagel. (It used to be a cup of "joe" and a jelly doughnut.) At the warehouse, they hear the horn and run for the snack wagon, grab a cup of coffee, and gather at the picnic table on the concrete floor. For the next few minutes, the gossipers hold court, tearing down the boss, or passing along rumors that the company is in trouble or that the supervisor in customer service is a homosexual.

Complaining means speaking against a *situation* or *person* without taking steps toward positive conflict resolution. The contemporary term for this habit is "whining."

"A malicious man disguises himself with his lips, but in his heart he harbors deceit. Though his speech is charming, do not believe him, for seven abominations fill his heart" (Proverbs 26:24–25).

Have you ever noticed how easily a tone of dissent can arise—almost unnoticed—in conversations at work? Talk of the supervisor's handling of personnel situations and job assignments moves from, "I wish he would do it differently" to "I don't think he'll ever do it right." Complaining is like a whisper between two conspirators. The complainer works in the shadows, causing problems or dissension. God's way is to work in the light, address the problem, and seek a solution.

Gossip involves sharing information or discussing problems with people who are not part of the problem or part of the solution. The military calls it "scuttlebutt." In the office or factory, it's the "grapevine." Gossip gives men a sense of control, of being on the "inside," and of winning favor by knowing more than others. Sometimes legitimate information is disseminated—but so are assumptions, rumors, and lies. Be wary of any information that comes to you in this manner. Because of the way gossip is passed from person to person, it's usually exaggerated, distorted, and full of misinformation by the time you hear it.

If you pick up information and repeat it without substantiation, you have participated in the destructive pastime of gossip.

Profanity and Coarse Language

Do you cringe when you hear the name of Jesus used in a profane manner? Having played competitive sports, lived in a fraternity, and been in the army, I have heard my share of foul words and coarse jokes. In many occupations, swearing, sexual innuendo, and crude humor is a way of life—a male rite of passage.

In our culture, coarse language has become the mark of a man. For some men, profanity begins early in life, following a role model. (Think about it, Dad.) It's a way to fit in with other guys. Actually, swearing reflects a lack of self-control, laziness in the use of the English language, and, I think, a lack of confidence. Sadly, it's not at all rare to find this behavior in Christian men.

As believers in the workplace, others look at our actions and words and judge them against our stated beliefs. The unbeliever who hears profanity and crude speech from us will judge if our "talk" matches our "walk."

Bill owned a small company, and asked me how he could expose his twenty employees to his faith in Christ. Bill had become a Christian later in life, and his previous manufacturing management jobs were in environments when profanity and crudeness were rampant. Several of these expressions lingered in his speech. As we talked I challenged Bill with the assignment of eliminating *all* of those old cuss words from his language.

For a period of two months he stopped using any swear words in his daily communication. It wasn't long before the crew in his company began to notice. On one occasion, one of his staff apologized for swearing in front of him. Bill had set a new standard for himself, and that influenced others. His self-control paid great dividends in his spiritual influence on his employees.

As Paul recommends, "Do not let any unwholesome talk come out of your mouths, but only what is helpful for building others up according to their needs, that it may benefit those who listen" (Ephesians 4:29).

Dealing With Criticism and Gossip

One great way to get rid of any negative habit is to replace it with a positive one. Here are some positive ways to use your tongue:

Giving a good report about *others*. Have you ever heard someone being complimented behind his back? Would it surprise you if someone came into the lunchroom and said, "Bob really did a great job on this project—I couldn't have finished on time without his extra effort." The ability to express ourselves in a supportive manner reflects strongly on our character and our willingness to be part of the team. Here are some ways we can spread some good news:

- Reverse gossip—say something positive about someone behind his back. Be honest; don't flatter.
- Tell the boss when someone has done a good job.
- Tell a customer or vendor about a positive experience with his staff.
- Pass along anything positive you may hear about someone else.

Giving a good report to *others*. Why is it that the simple words "thank you" are so underused in the workplace today? The majority of people I talk with feel unappreciated by their boss and the people around them. In dealing with our children, we're told we should give ten positives for every negative remark. How would following this principle change the atmosphere where you work? It would begin to sound like this:

- "Thanks for your help."
- "Mary, that report looks great. Thanks for staying late to finish it."
- "Steve, your punctuality has really improved since our talk. Thanks for the effort you're making."
- "Helen, have I told you recently how much I appreciate all the work you do? You make my job much easier."
- "Mike, that was an outstanding piece of work on the last proposal."

Overusing good reports can become flattery *or* manipulation. But genuine expressions of affirmation for good work—even if it is part of the job description—are always welcome. Criticism and gossip can't live long in a positive atmosphere.

What's Your Part?

In dealing with negative language, the first step is to diagnose your level of participation. Here are the possibilities:

You are an initiator. The initiator will often get the ball rolling. He comes in each morning with the latest off-color joke. He starts the conversation at lunch with, "You'll never believe the stupid thing Jones did today!" Some of us may come across information we know others will enjoy and can't resist passing it along.

If you are the one who usually starts conversations like this, you may be an initiator.

You are a responder. When J. R. tells his daily off-color joke, and you join in the laughter or add a dirty joke of your own, you are a responder. The responder will listen to the gossip or criticism, make a comment or two, and even seek *more* details. Natural human curiosity can be a powerful force, and you may find yourself being drawn into conversations like this.

You ignore inappropriate talk. As a new Christian I received this advice from a trusted friend: "Refusing to laugh at an off-color joke may be one of the hardest things you have to do." This act of silence may be very important to someone else who has felt as you do but doesn't have your courage.

Sometimes it's enough to simply remain silent in the presence of gossip or crude talk. If the conversation is taking place where you can hear it, but does not directly involve you, this may be the best choice. If you are new on the job, it may be necessary for you to be silent until you're able to build relationships and credibility in order to confront the situation more directly. At times you may need to physically remove yourself from the group in order to avoid appearing to participate by your presence.

You confront the situation. Confrontation may mean nothing more than asking a simple question, "Have you verified that with Bill?" Or, "Does John know how you feel?" Sometimes a light response such as, "My ears are burning," may be a subtle way of pointing out foul language.

Certainly, if you are in a position of responsibility, you can be more direct with the people you manage. Perhaps you can call attention to their language by reminding them of the image the company wants to project to customers and other professionals.

By far, the most powerful thing you can do is to set a good and consistent example.

Steps to Take When You're the Problem

- Admit to yourself and to God that you have a problem with criticism, gossip, or profanity.
- Write down the nature of the problem. List the possible consequences of continuing to use negative speech.
- Commit to making a change. Go before the Lord daily and ask Him to take away the desire to be critical, speak inappropriately, or swear.
- Write down the specific actions you want to change: "I will say only positive things to my secretary for one week." Concentrate on eliminating swear words. "I will stop in the middle of any gossip that I initiate." Put notes in your daily planner, on your work bench, or on

the bathroom mirror at home.

- If crude jokes are your downfall, do some research. Learn some funny *clean* jokes, and begin to tell them.
- Ask a friend to hold you accountable, giving him permission to alert you to or remind you of words misspoken.
- Ask forgiveness from those in your work environment—or elsewhere—whom you may have offended. Seek counsel from a pastor or friend to confirm that this step is appropriate.

Wisdom About Confronting Others

Directly confronting another person about his or her language is a sensitive issue. It's always a risk, with no guarantees that there will be a positive result. Men can become angry, defensive, or clam up. It's certainly not something to be done lightly or frequently. Usually if you set a consistent example, drop a few hints, and wait patiently, you'll begin to see changes in those around you.

But there may be situations in which a more direct conversation is necessary; if so, take the following steps:

- How is your behavior? Perhaps you need to deal with the "log in your own eye" first.
- Define your purpose. Is a biblical standard being violated? Is there any pride on your part?
- Do you have a relationship with the person to be confronted? This is the basis for getting results.
- Be prepared to name times and places where you heard him swear, gossip, or criticize. Give examples of what occurred and the impact the words had on you.
- Pray about the meeting. Ask God to prepare the heart of

your co-worker and to give you a spirit of peace, unity, and love—not judgment.

The book of James describes the tongue as powerful. Even though it is a very small part of the body, it can set the course of our lives. An Indian proverb states, "Whatever you are full of will spill out when you are bumped." What we say in unguarded moments of anger or frustration is an indication of who we really are on the inside.

We can call on God's power to help us create new habit patterns in speech. And as we bring our tongue under control, we can be sure that we are maturing and becoming more like Christ.

For Thought and Discussion

1. Do you have problems with negative co-workers in your work area?
2. Where do you stand with the four listed categories of participation?
3. Do you need to confront someone in the workplace who is poisoning the atmosphere of the office?

Conflict #9:
When Your Work Takes Over Your Life

Have you ever heard these questions from your wife?

- "Why do you always have to work Saturdays?"
- "Would it ever be possible for us to have dinner by six o'clock again?"
- "Honey, you're tired. Don't you think you've been pushing it?"
- "Why can't we take a ten-day vacation?"
- "Work! Work! Work! Why can't you and I have more time together?"
- "Sweetie, is it possible you could spend more time with the kids?"
- "Are you *too* tired again tonight?"

Maybe you've asked yourself some of the same questions, or, "What in the world am I doing working all the time? There has to be more to life than this!" For some guys, working too much leads to guilt or personal dissatisfaction. Co-workers may wonder what you are "trying to prove," which can cause relationship conflicts with them.

Some men work too much because the company *requires* fifty- or sixty-hour weeks almost as a condition of employment. Many construction, software, and manufacturing companies expect their employees to put in extra time. If working long hours is not your choice, then apply what you learned in the chapter on leaving a job. This chapter deals primarily with those of us who *choose* to work more hours than is healthy for our emotions, health, and family.

People who put in excessive hours are often referred to as "workaholics." I don't like the term because it implies a condition out of your control—something caused by an outside force. Sometimes it refers to a driven man, climbing the corporate ladder with no regard for anyone else. But many of us are normal guys who love our family—it's just that we've made overwork a habit. And now we want to do something about it.

If your time card or datebook is full to overflowing, if you bring home work every night, or if you think about work all the time, you may have a problem. I call those of us with this work problem "leisure impaired."

How Much Work Is Too Much?

We have to be careful in defining who works too much. There are no "job" referees to make a judgment call if you work forty hours and ten minutes. My good friend Ollie works sixty hours a week or more, and still has time for a date with his wife, personal prayer, coaching his son's Little League team, and visiting new members of the church. Another acquaintance, Bill, finds forty hours of work is all he can handle, *period*. Factors such as natural energy level, passion for your work, happiness, and personal support at home can all impact the definition of how much work is enough and how much is too much.

We become unbalanced when the time and energy we expend on the work side of our life exceeds an acceptable standard. This standard will be different for each person. But when our preoccupation with work begins to negatively impact our relationship with family, God, and friends, and when it takes us away from other responsibilities, we are out of balance.

Two Types of Leisure-Impaired Men

I like to classify leisure-impaired men in two categories: the *strivers* and the *arrivers*.

The Striver. The striver is consumed by work, trying to prove his worth by seeking favor with others, avoiding failure, searching for fame and fortune, trying to keep up with technology, or still trying to win a critical father's approval. Often he has no time to enjoy the process or the fruits of his labor. He finishes one job and immediately sets another goal. The striver believes his value is tied up in what he does, not who he is. His mood will be high when he does well and low when he has not met his own expectations.

William was consistently at his desk a half-hour before starting time and an hour after work. He admitted to me that he wanted his managers to see him at his desk—committed and loyal. He also used the extra time to prepare reports, covering every angle so that he would never be wrong. This added about ten hours a week to his schedule. William is a striver.

The Arriver. You may know this man. He spends extra hours at work because he loves what he's doing, not because he is trying to prove something. He has arrived. Work is fun, the time flies by, and the results he achieves are satisfying. His job has all the elements of passion and significance we discussed in chapter 2. There is only one problem—his wife, kids, family, and friends want and need more of his time and attention.

Alex was a manufacturing master technician who loved his work and arrived early because he always had a project to complete. He was also a mentor to younger workers and a source of knowledge for others in the company. Most days he didn't have time to get all his regular work done, so he stayed a little longer after the whistle blew. Alex and his wife met with me because a problem was brewing—she was feeling neglected, and the children hardly ever saw their father.

There are several reasons why a man becomes a striver or an arriver:

- A parent has modeled excessive work.
- Working too much has become a habit.
- You are trying—consciously or unconsciously—to prove your value to someone.
- You have a high energy level, requiring constant activity.
- You feel insecure in your abilities.
- Work enables you to avoid problems at home.
- You *want* a higher standard of living than you *need*.
- You crave the prestige of going higher and higher in your career, or the power you will have if you achieve a higher position.

Both *strivers* and *arrivers* can be highly successful from a work standpoint, but highly unsuccessful in other areas of their lives. Consulting with both types, I've noticed in many a deep yearning to change the status quo and get off the work locomotive.

Symptoms of the Leisure-Impaired Man

Denial is a big issue with a lot of us. It was with me. "I'm not consumed with work, I just love what I do, and it's the

only way to get ahead." I actually believed that line for a
long time. Do any of the following attributes of the leisure-
impaired man apply to you?

- putting in a "few more hours" to get the job done right
  or on time
- working to get a head start on current projects so you
  can slow down "next month"
- preparing with great detail so that no one can challenge
  the premise, the results, the system, the plan, or the pre-
  senter (Some refer to this as perfectionism.)
- consumed with meeting the deadlines, cost estimates,
  and promises (sometimes unrealistic) made to customers, vendors, managers
- taking on more assignments to build additional responsibility, to obtain more job evaluation points, or to gain
  recognition
- volunteering to take on another assignment to show the
  management how much you can do
- loving the feeling of being "on a roll" with an idea, design, story, problem to be solved
- giving a higher priority to work than anything else in
  life
- taking a "few" papers home for the weekend, or one key
  document on your vacation—and then turning down a
  few waterskiing runs to finish up the last proposal
- constantly thinking about work at home, in the car, and
  in church
- taking three- or four-day vacations (no time for a two-
  week extended trip)
- canceling vacation plans because something comes up
  at work
- hurrying visitors out of the house so you can reach for
  the mouse and work on that report, or get over to the
  shop and finish a project

- need to make some additional money while the opportunity is there (overtime, more sales calls, two or three more projects)
- realizing you can't make it financially without the overtime

Each of us will have one or two symptoms, perhaps more, during a crisis period. But if you are consumed with work, you will evidence many of these traits consistently. If you want to know whether you are "leisure-impaired," read this list to your wife or trusted friend. They'll know.

The Traveling Briefcase/ Toolbox—Bringing Work Home

Gail watches the love of her life leave the garage as he heads toward the house, leaving footprints in the snow. She looks at the clock . . . 6:25. She knows he'll be tired, and dinner is ready. And then her heart sinks . . . *He's got that briefcase with him again!* He left before daybreak, and Gail knows he needs some rest—but she also wonders, *When are we going to have some time to talk about Billy's behavior and Andrea's grades. . . ?*

The Mental Briefcase/Toolbox.
Strivers and arrivers also come home with their mind filled with challenges and problems from work. The other day I was sitting in church thinking about a client. (God forgive me.) With a start, I returned to the present as 500 people laughed at a point made by the pastor. Turning to Jeanne, I asked, "What's so funny?" She knew where my mind had been.

Wives and children have a legitimate complaint when work is constantly on our minds. In the midst of a TV program, newspaper story, or even a conversation, our work-consciousness suddenly activates, *Remember that phone call to Jones tomorrow.* (My good friend Chuck Snyder thinks employers find a way to implant a computer chip in our brains that makes us think about work!)

A Special Case—The Small Business Owner

John is the owner of a small retail business. As janitor, bill payer/collector, marketing executive, operations manager, and long-range planner, his mind constantly moves back and forth on all fronts. Then he has to take definitive action such as adding or removing staff, expanding or contracting operations, managing cash flow—not to mention getting the bills out on time. John and thousands of other owners are the financial backbone of America. But the personal price of ownership can be high. Many hours are spent working and thinking about business.

Judging from the number of calls I get from wives, many of these men are leisure-impaired. John's wife, Ellen, called with this problem: "My husband is consumed with his work. For the number of hours he puts in, his effective hourly rate must be $6.00 or $7.00. We need some help."

Another woman called to say, "I need Mike to be home more often. Even though the money is good and he seems happy, our family life is nonexistent."

Men like John and Mike spend many hours building their business as a labor of love. Whether they're making money is often not as important as building their dream.

Some small business owners handle the pressure extremely well. For others, the pressure builds like a boiler with a faulty safety valve—pressure to sell, deliver service, pay the bills, manage employees. Here are some reasons why men may hang on to their own business too long:

• They don't want to come under the authority of a boss (rebellion).

- They're not sure they can make it in the real world (personal insecurity).
- They refuse to work for someone else—as if that means they've failed (pride).

The small business owner must constantly seek God's direction in starting, keeping, or closing down a business. If you cannot get beyond the long hours at work and mental distraction at home, think about getting a "regular job."

Important Is As Important Does

Men ultimately base their actions on what's important to them. Josh has a standing basketball game on Thursday that he never misses. On the other hand, he frequently sleeps late on Sunday and misses church. He *says* church is important to him—but what do his actions say?

Each one of us prioritizes activities, people, and thoughts according to their importance. Choices made over time become our values. If you ask yourself where you spend your *time, treasure, talents*, and *thoughts*, you will have defined your actual values. If we say that our family is our top priority, but we spend all our time and energy at work, then we allow our choices to shape our values. The challenge is to identify our values first, and then base our priorities on that standard.

Recently, the light came on for me as the result of a conversation with my wife. I'd planned to call some friends to get some information for our son Jeff, who was coming home from the Midwest. She reminded me about this twice. On an evening, two days prior to Jeff's arrival, I was sitting at the computer, happily engaged in writing, when Jeanne asked, "Have you made the calls yet?" I replied, "No." To which she responded abruptly, "Obviously this is not very important to you!"

Being the strong, mature Christian that I am, I went to my first line of defense. "It is important to me, don't say that it isn't." *My mistake!*

Jeanne answered, "If it were important to you, you would have made the calls. If Jeff were a client you would have made the calls." It took me a day to realize that Jeanne was not only right but she had hit upon a very important principle.

As I thought through my response to Jeanne, the *perceived value* of the calls was high, but the *actual value* was much lower than it should have been. If these calls had been to significant customers, I would have made them immediately and without reminders. The same holds true for the time you spend with your work. If reducing your hours on the job is important, you will find a way to do it by rescheduling, cutting back, or finding new employment.

Overwork doesn't need to mean lack of love or commitment. It would be a great error to say that strivers and arrivers don't love their wives, families, or God. But the truth is, men, we can mentally assent to our commitment but still carry on with unhealthy work patterns. Our actions don't reflect our good intentions.

You must decide if changing your work habits is important. If it is, then change is possible. If it is not, then real change probably won't happen. Many of us haven't been taught how to lead a balanced life, how to recognize when we are out of balance, or how to make needed changes.

Change Is Up to You

If you choose to leave a compulsive, unhealthy work style behind, you will be engaged in a battle against three forces:

• the world (everybody is working hard);

- the flesh (I want that promotion);
- and the devil (it's okay, just another hour).

The way out starts with God. Confess to Him your over-commitment toward work and ask for His help. Do the following:

- Establish a consistent prayer time and ask God for help in changing.
- Ask for a new vision of a balanced life.
- Memorize Psalm 1.
- Pray with your wife and ask for her insight about values and priorities.
- Pray with another man for accountability.
- Acknowledge that God can stretch your time and bring in the business, help solve the problems, and find someone else to serve the church or ministry, allowing you to work a "normal" schedule.

Reestablish your value structure.
Take an inventory of the five most important things in your life and see how much time you are spending with each. Prioritize the following list:

Time with friends	Security
Peace of mind	Retirement account
Money	Time with your parents
Health	Time with God
Recognition	Sports
Travel	Time with your children
Ministry	Vacations, recreation
Job success/advancement	Time with your wife

Now ask yourself these questions: Does the way I spend my time reflect these values? Would someone observing me clearly see these priorities?

Establish accountability.

Breaking habits can take time. You will need someone to support, coach, and pray for you. Establish this relationship with another man, and give him permission to ask about your progress.

- Commit that you will be obedient and subject to accountability in making the move to a more balanced life.
- Verbally, or in writing, commit to your family that you will change.

Planning

Replacing negative patterns will be easier if you take steps that will encourage change. Plan your work schedule for one month in advance:

- Schedule yourself to leave the office, warehouse, or lab on time.
- Don't make decisions at the point of decision. Decide before the need comes up how much extra time you are willing to put in and when that time will be.
- Outline your plans to change your schedule. Discuss your new plans with your manager, subordinates, or board of directors. Ask for their support.
- Make a commitment not to take work home. (Start with two days a week if necessary.)

Plan your personal activities for one month.

- Make a list of non-work activities for the month.
- Schedule family activities, personal time with God, social and leisure activities. Put them in your appointment book or buy one just for non-work activities.
- Schedule a surprise weekend with your wife. *You plan it.*

These are incremental steps in breaking the habit of being leisure-impaired. Do it a step at a time and, slowly, important changes will take place in your life.

If you suffer from the conflict of *work versus family*, read Psalm 1:3. If you are, as the psalm says, "planted by streams of water," then "whatever you do prospers." You don't *have* to make a choice between a successful career and a successful family. God delights to give you both—if you will order your priorities according to His Word. We demonstrate a lack of trust in God when we work too long or too hard over an extended period of time.

Decide what is important and be a good steward of the energy resources God has given you. Change won't occur overnight. But take the first steps: As the Nike commercials say, *Just do it*. In the words of an anonymous business philosopher, "No man on his deathbed has ever said, 'I wish I'd spent more time at the office.' "

For Thought and Discussion

1. Do you work too much? If so, are you a *striver* or an *arriver?*
2. How do your wife and family feel about your work schedule?
3. Have you determined what your values are?
4. Does your life reflect those values?
5. Make a choice: if your assessment reveals you to be leisure-impaired, have you decided it's important enough for you to change?

Conflict #10: Sharing Your Faith at Work

Sarah was a talented secretary in our department. But recently her energy seemed low and her previously outgoing personality had become a dark cloud. I asked Sarah if there was a problem she'd like to talk about. Her immediate response was, "Yes."

As she talked about two difficult circumstances in her life, the tears flowed. One of the issues was a personal problem she was feeling very guilty about.

Now I had a conflict myself. Should I talk to her about God's grace and forgiveness? I didn't know where she stood with matters of faith. Maybe I should be a friend and offer only practical advice. Since I was one of the managers she reported to, I had concerns about putting pressure on her. Would this be taking advantage of a difficult personal situation? Is there such a thing as religious harassment? For a couple of days I prayed and agonized about it.

Finally I made my decision. I asked Sarah if she would like to have a cup of coffee and began the conversation like this, "Sarah, stop me at any time, but I want to talk about something I think might help you right now—that is God's grace and forgiveness." She listened intently, and kept asking me to continue.

The short version of a long story is that over a period of months she established a relationship with Jesus Christ. She solved the problems that had been bothering her, and we were able to maintain both a friendship and a professional relationship. For some men my decision and that dialogue may have been easy. But even after twenty years, I struggle with when and how to share my faith in a direct and effective manner, especially in the work environment.

Have you ever been in a similar situation at the office or in the shop? Perhaps there is a perfect opening for you to put in a word about God's faithfulness, and you freeze. Your mind starts a running dialogue with your heart: *Should I say anything? Is it really appropriate? What if I say the wrong thing? What if I offend him? What if he thinks I'm weird?*

Then maybe your mind jumps right to the Book of Revelation: "I know your deeds, that you are neither cold nor hot. I wish that you were either one or the other! So, because you are lukewarm—neither hot nor cold—I am about to spit you out of my mouth" (Revelation 3:15–16). Now besides the confusion of what to do, you may have some guilt about not taking the opportunity to encourage a believer, or to "plant a seed" with someone new. Where is that line between rushing in "where angels fear to tread" and the Great Commission? Conflicts at work are not always between people, but may begin in our minds and hearts.

Most of us have experienced the sweaty palms when an opening to speak about faith came about—then doubt and guilt as the opportunity passed by. Some of us can also remember the joy when we took the risk and a co-worker responded favorably. Sharing our knowledge and understanding of God can take place on two fronts:

- introducing people to God's love and power
- encouraging another believer to grow spiritually

My mentors, during my early Christian experience, gave me two pieces of advice: "If God puts someone on your doorstep, respond to their need." And, "The need is not the call." In other words, just seeing someone in need does not mean you should jump in. But you should put your antennae up and look for people who may be curious about God, who are reaching out for help, or who may want to hear your story.

Why the Conflict in Sharing Our Faith?

Mike was working next to Sam as they finished the wiring on a major construction project. They'd been working together about three months, and the two of them had hit it off pretty well. Over the past week, Sam had been talking about some problems with his live-in girlfriend. Mike finally felt compelled to share a biblical truth. "Sam, I think you ought to get married, or get out of the relationship. I'm not here to judge you, but God has been important in my life, and one of His principles is that living together if you're not married is not right."

Over the next several weeks, Mike was surprised at Sam's openness. He brought up questions about how to have a relationship with God and how to find a good church, and what happens to people who die without ever hearing about Jesus. At Mike's suggestion, he contacted a pastor for help with problems he was having with his girlfriend's teenage son.

Then one day, out of the blue, Sam said, "She said *yes*."

Mike asked, "Who said *yes*, to *what*?"

"My girlfriend said she wanted to get married, and we set the date," Sam replied.

Sam is now married, and has begun to attend church. Mike took the opportunity to initiate a conversation that paid some eternal dividends.

Most men are somewhat guarded about personal communication in general—and talking about God in particular. Men don't want to interfere in another man's life without some just cause. The risk factor in our minds can produce anxieties such as the fear of

- turning people off toward you and the gospel;
- rejection and/or social disapproval;
- being classified by co-workers as a religious fanatic;
- not knowing the Bible and its principles;
- not doing a good job of speaking about your faith;
- impact on career growth opportunities;
- previous experiences with sharing faith that were negative;
- interfering in the lives of others.

All of these anxieties are understandable and real. Those who find the whole process difficult need encouragement and training, not criticism. The following pages are designed to respond to this troublesome conflict for men at work.

What Is Your Role?

The Scriptures are clear that we are to model our faith before others: make disciples, be salt and light, love our neighbor. God wants His people to share the wealth of His love with the world of co-workers, customers, and vendors. We need to encourage each other to be bold in our efforts. I am a Christian today because another man took the time and some risk in explaining to me why Jesus died for my sins and how I could live at peace with God.

Sometimes we may plant the seed of faith for the first time. Other times we will water what has been planted by another man. And at other times we'll harvest and actually introduce someone to God.

In his book *Your Spiritual Gifts*, Peter Wagner defines a spiritual gift as "a special attribute given by the Holy Spirit to every member of the Body of Christ according to God's grace . . ." One of those gifts is *evangelism*. Many of us admire the evangelist in the workplace who confidently shares the gospel and brings others to a commitment to Christ. You may or may not have a gift of evangelism.

Some of us have gifts that are just as important that will be used in a different manner to accomplish the same goal. Those with the spiritual gifts of help, mercy, or encouragement may find different ways to express the hope they see in the Lord. No one's good at everything, but everyone is good at something. Find out what your gifts are and use them to spread the Good News.

Attitude

Attitude is not something that just happens to you. It is something you cultivate by deliberate actions and decisions. In major league baseball, a good shortstop takes the field every inning with the desire to have a ball hit to him so he can make the play. A good hitter wants to be up when the bases are loaded with two outs and the game on the line. Could these players excel without this attitude? I doubt it.

On Sunday the pastor spoke about sharing your faith and here it is Monday morning. Instead of looking forward to who God might put on your doorstep today, you're hoping no one will bring up anything that might put you on the spot. Can you effectively represent your faith with this attitude? How can you develop the right attitude? You need to become aware of three things: anticipation, availability and awareness.

Anticipation

I was a tournament handball player in my younger days and looked forward to playing in a championship game. I would think about the game, develop a strategy, and have a few "butterflies" before the first point. There is no reason why we can't anticipate with equal joy and intensity an opportunity to share the gospel. But instead of anticipation, there is often fear, confusion, and avoidance. To develop this anticipation, you need to prepare.

Just as the baseball player practices before the game and prepares himself for many different situations, you need to prepare to witness effectively. If responding to the opportunities you have is important, then you will take time to prepare. Often the difference between anticipation and avoidance is *confidence*. Preparation will give you this confidence.

Another key to anticipation is prayer. Ask God to bring someone to you today with whom you can share your faith on some level. Then anticipate that He will do just that. When I was a new Christian, I needed help finishing a project and asked a colleague for assistance. He answered, "I prayed this morning that I would be able to help someone today. I'd be *glad* to!" I later found out that he was under pressure of a deadline himself, but because he saw my request as a direct answer to his prayer, he responded positively. What a powerful lesson that was to me!

Awareness

It's easy to get so focused on our work during the day that we tune out everything else. It is possible to raise our awareness of those around us by making a conscious effort to do so. As I get older (mature), I try to respond to every new person that enters my business life with a question, "Lord, is this person part of my call? If so, show me how." If you have a loved one who is struggling with his faith, wouldn't it be great if thousands of men were asking that question and just one happened to encounter him in the workplace?

Just as Jesus didn't heal everyone, we are not called to witness to everyone. As we pray, God will make it clear where our responsibility lies. Some of the telltale signs are someone who

- asks about your faith and what it means to you;
- talks about reading materials that include religious themes;
- discusses personal problems.

If you raise your awareness and look for places to join God where He is already at work in someone's life, you will be amazed at how easy sharing your faith can be.

Availability

We all work under the pressure of deadlines, quotas, and appointments. Being "too busy" is a wonderful excuse for not taking an opportunity that comes up. Certainly we want to balance a desire to share our faith with our employer's right to expect a full day's work. Here are some times when we can be available:

- breaks, such as coffee or lunch
- driving to appointments, or to jobsites
- when traveling on business with a colleague
- before or after work

If a wonderful opening comes up at an inappropriate time, it is perfectly all right to respond with, "I'd really like to talk about this further. Could we meet for lunch tomorrow?" Or, "How about getting together this weekend to fin-

ish this discussion?" While at work, we are a "guest" in the
owner's house or the customer's business. We owe the man
a fair day's work at the highest quality. Proclaiming the gospel at the expense of deadlines, production, and operational matters is not only bad business, it is counter to
God's principles against stealing (time).

Building Confidence

Find a mentor.

A mentor is someone who can show you the ropes. One
of my mentors is Chuck Snyder, who owns his own advertising business. He has been a model and an encouragement
for me in sharing my faith. He and his wife, Barb, have led
Bible studies for the players and coaches of the Seahawks,
the Mariners, and teams at the University of Washington.
Chuck can't stand "religiosity" and moves into the business world with the attitude, "I'm just an ordinary guy with
my own problems, but I have some pretty good solutions.
Wanna listen?" I have learned much from his stories, suc-
cesses—and yes, a few things that didn't turn out. Here is
one example of a success:

Chuck befriended a man at a company with which he
did business. Over the course of several conversations, he
confirmed that Herschel was Jewish. Chuck sent him cards
on his birthday and in celebration of Hanukkah and took
time to ask about Herschel's family. They had some light-
hearted debates about Jesus and whether or not He was the
Messiah.

Eventually Herschel transferred out of the area, but
Chuck kept the cards going. One day, a note from Herschel
arrived saying that "he had accepted the fact that a Jewish
carpenter from Bethlehem died for him." Chuck had faith-
fully talked about Christ, and someone led Herschel into
God's kingdom.

Prior to my becoming a tournament handball player, my volunteer mentor/coach, Bob Bunch, spent hours teaching me position, shots, and tricks of the game. You need this same type of coaching in order to share your faith at work. Gathering ideas and hearing successful stories from someone who has been there is a good place to start, but this does not happen by accident. Seek out a businessman who has been successful in integrating his faith with his work and ask for coaching, guidance, and ideas. You can also ask your pastor for advice or talk to a man whom you respect in your church.

Training

Most churches offer classes on evangelism from time to time. Seek out one of these, or ask your pastor for materials he may have on this subject. These classes not only give you a good foundation for how and when to share your faith, but they also frequently give you a sample "script" to practice. Another source of inspiration is stories of men who have taken their faith into the workplace and made a difference. (A list of some helpful books is included in the Bibliography.)

God's Word is also a great source of *information* as well as *inspiration*. Information is the basis for knowing God's plan and character. Inspiration provides encouragement to take a risk and share that information. Reading the Word with anticipation suggests that today you will find an opportunity to apply what you've read. When God has spoken to me through a Scripture or Bible story, frequently I have occasion to share that insight with several people during the week.

Examine Your Own Experience and Beliefs About God

I am amazed by the number of long-time believers who have their doubts about God's reality, His presence, and His

power. Many don't discuss their beliefs with others because they aren't sure what they believe. The following exercises provide a basis for understanding what you believe.
They will help you analyze your own walk of faith and provide a foundation of information to discuss with others.

- Write down the times when you sensed God's presence
  particularly close to you. Write out the circumstances,
  your feelings, and how you sensed God's closeness.
- List times when you received an answer to prayer that
  you know only God could have orchestrated. Detail the
  situations, your requests, and the answers that were received.
- Start a journal to record God's activities in your life, including prayer requests, answers, and miracles.
- Write the story of your personal walk with God and con-
  version—your testimony. Include any rebellion or times
  of disinterest, your eventual move to a decision to trust
  Christ, and the impact it has had on your life.

A Special Tribute

I will always be in debt to Tom Glover, my new neighbor
and fledgling attorney (now Judge Glover). We worked in
the same building downtown and made the commute together for several years. He always seemed to be interested
in what I was doing, my family, my work, and participation
in amateur sports. He also enjoyed talking about business
and world events. One day he tied some current events hap-
pening in the Mideast with some interesting history about
the same area. Over time I began to enjoy his stories about
the Crusaders, Jerusalem, and even about prophecy.

Tom found out in short order that I knew little about biblical history or God. Yet all our conversations seemed so
natural, just another part of our relationship. One evening

as I dropped him off at his house, he announced, "Gretchen and I are praying for you and Jeanne." I went home, told Jeanne, and she said, "And we aren't even sick!" Soon thereafter, they invited us to church, and within a year I had accepted Christ and Jeanne had recommitted her life to Him. Today our three children, my parents, and several other family members are believers. Our lives were changed forever. Thanks, Tom!

What Tom did with me can be a model for all of us. Tom

- built a relationship with me;
- showed interest in me;
- personalized his belief and related it to today's world;
- never pressured me or went "for the kill";
- asked me, "Do you want to know more?";
- waited for the Holy Spirit's timing before talking about God.

Some Cautions

A situation that requires discretion is witnessing from a position of authority within your company. Whether you are a foreman, crew leader, department manager, or vice-president, you never want employees to feel they are being subject to any form of "blackmail." In this day and age of court-mandated anti-discrimination, you need to be sure that your motives are not misunderstood.

This means bending over backward to treat each person under your authority equally, regardless of whatever personal views they may hold. As you seek God's wisdom, He can, and will, direct your responses to meet an individual's need without compromising your position legally.

Paying a Price

Even if your approach is low-key and sensitive, you may experience some rejection. I was hired by an electronics company to help Betty transition out of the company due to a layoff. As we talked, Betty expressed her new faith in God and presented a problem she was currently experiencing with another person. I told her of my faith and gave her a biblical approach to resolving her conflict. She was so excited that she went back and told the Human Resources director how much I had helped her.

The next day I received a blunt call from the director, saying, "I didn't hire you to be a pastor. I hired you to be career counselor."

Although I never received any more business from that company, I still feel that what I did was appropriate in that situation. I am thankful that one day my knee will bow before God and not that Human Resources director.

Nothing exceeds the blessing of moving someone closer to, further along, or into God's kingdom. If you ask, God will bring people who need to grow in faith. For those of you who haven't made furthering the kingdom a priority, why not explore how to start now? Ask God to help. Go slow, but go. Each of us can experience the reward of sharing the Good News at work, and we need to encourage each other to step out. For you men who are regularly sharing your faith, continue the good work and be available to mentor and teach others.

Our pastor, Ken Hutcherson, interjects in his services weekly, "Our challenge is to populate heaven—and depopulate hell."

For Thought and Discussion

1. Do you need more courage to share your faith?
2. Who might you talk with that could help and encourage you?
3. Do you have a person in mind who you would like to introduce to Jesus Christ? What's your next step?

Summary:
Making It Happen

It's Sunday night, and you've just finished the preceding chapters. Tomorrow is Monday. You're about to return to a dead-end job, an irritating co-worker, or a terrible boss. Is there anything that you are going to do differently because of the information you have? Your answer to this question will depend on three things: your *attitude*, your *access to God*, and your *action*.

Attitude

Diamonds are lumps of coal that have been under a lot of pressure for an extended period of time. Inspirational speakers use this example over and over again to show that trials can change us for the better. The apostle James doesn't mince words when it comes to the value of attitude in handling conflict:

"Consider it pure joy, my brothers, whenever you face trials of many kinds, because you know that the testing of your faith develops perseverance" (James 1:2–3).

When I was faced with a dead end in my job several years ago, the last thing I wanted to do was say, "Wow, thanks, God, for the testing. I find great joy in this." But I've learned that giving thanks is the right thing to do regardless of how I feel.

Now I look at most problems and know that getting my attitude right is a big part of the solution. Do I do it right every time? No. But I also recognize very quickly when I am feeling sorry for myself. Once I take the focus off myself and put it on God, it's amazing how my attitude changes. Focusing on myself, I see only my human limitations, previous failures, and doubt. Focusing on God, I see His power, omniscience, and love.

The word "perseverance" implies living through an uncomfortable situation for an extended period of time. I guess that's where the diamond thing comes in to play. So how do we change our attitude?

One of the best ways I know is by giving thanks, and here is what the Bible says about that:

"Rejoice! Let your gentleness be evident to all. The Lord is near. Do not be anxious about anything, but in everything, by prayer and petition, with thanksgiving, present your requests to God. And the peace of God, which transcends all understanding, will guard your hearts and your minds in Christ Jesus" (Philippians 4:4–7).

What I notice about this Scripture is that it doesn't say we have to be thankful *for* everything. That's a big relief—because it would sure be a stretch for me to be thankful for things like a job I hate or a boss who hasn't said a kind word to me for over a year. But as I present my requests to God for a new job or a different supervisor, I can give thanks for facts I know to be true—that He will use these difficulties for my good, that He has a plan even though I can't see it, that He will be with me all the way, and that He is guiding me to the way out.

I never met a cookie I didn't like. My first reaction when I see a plate of chocolate chip or peanut butter cookies is to grab one and eat it. Jeanne thinks my hand has a cookie magnet, a fact that has caused her to hide the cookies in some very creative places. My cookie eating has no connection to a feeling of hunger, it is an instinctive reaction: see cookie, eat cookie. I am trying to make my reaction to conflict just as instinctive: See problem, give thanks.

Access to God

I watched a demonstration of computer technology the other day that left me amazed. I was attending a meeting with a client involving several district managers. The Information Systems manager turned to the manager of a district two thousand miles away and said, "Would you like to see what your secretary is working on right now?" With the push of a couple keys, her computer screen appeared and we saw the letter she was typing. He told us that on her screen she would see the words, "You are being accessed." I'll bet she was glad she wasn't playing solitaire while the boss was gone!

When we are facing difficult challenges, God encourages us to access Him, and in return to make ourselves accessible to Him.

One of the best ways to access God is to dialogue with Him as you confront your internal and external conflicts. As I drive, I frequently find myself mulling over ideas and problems, talking to God. His Spirit lives within us, and He is called the Counselor and Comforter. You may be driving to a jobsite, feeding pages into the copy machine, or waiting for an appointment. Anytime, anyplace, you can access God simply by beginning a dialogue.

The nice thing about a dialogue with God is that you can be completely honest and tell Him how you feel. He won't be shocked. He already knows anyway. You can simply say, "Lord, I want to solve this personality clash with Randy— but I need some ideas in quick order. I'm at the end of my rope." Just tell it like it is, and then see if you don't find yourself "accessed" in return.

Take Action

At some point, we have to decide that the status quo is not acceptable and make a decision to change. Frequently, there is some risk involved in this decision.

One of my favorite stories in the Bible is in John 11, the story of Lazarus being raised from the dead. As you may recall, when Jesus arrived on the scene, Lazarus had been dead for four days and his sisters were bemoaning the fact that Jesus had arrived too late to heal him. So Jesus asked them to take action: roll the stone away from the entrance to his tomb. Mary and Martha had a very practical reason why this would not be a good idea: the smell. When they objected, Jesus said, "Did I not tell you that if you believed, you would see the glory of God?" Faced with that challenge, they did the smart thing and rolled away the stone. With that act of obedience, Jesus called to Lazarus, who immediately came out of the tomb.

In this story *belief* equaled *action*. Jesus wasn't asking for some intellectual assent to who He was or what He could do. They had to risk. It is important to note that the action they took did not solve their problem. They rolled away the stone and Lazarus was still dead. But their action allowed Jesus to act, to perform the miracle that solved their problem.

Think about this story when you're confronted with the need to act in the face of conflict. Most of the steps outlined for resolving problems in the previous chapters involve some degree of risk. Sometimes your wife or prayer partner may give you some advice that sounds just as crazy as rolling the stone away. Maybe like Mary and Martha you have some very persuasive reasons based on human logic or past experience why you don't want to take that action. If so, read John 11:40 again, and ask yourself what miracle of God you may miss out on if you choose not to step out in obedience and faith.

Conflict Has a Purpose

I had no idea that when I hit a dead end in my job and was deep in lethargy that God had a plan for that experience. Some twenty years later I would sit with many men who would describe the same condition. I could readily understand what they were saying, identify with their emotions, and give them hope. When the frustration of internal and external conflict in your work life becomes overwhelming, you can thank God for the bigger purpose, which may be to

- draw you closer to Him;
- allow you to see His power, which will bring trust in the future;
- show you where you need to change;
- help you mature spiritually and professionally;
- give you experience that you can use later to benefit others.

The message is clear: God has a perfect answer for every conflict we face—if we have the faith and obedience to seek it out. If we will choose the right attitude, turn to Him, and then take action, He will turn all those stumbling blocks we encounter at work into stepping stones. When things look terrible, remember what Paul wrote in Romans: "And we know that in all things God works for the good of those who

love him, who have been called according to his purpose"
(Romans 8:28).

A Real Life Example

In 1972, a unique individual by the name of Wayne Alderson took bold steps to solve a conflict of major proportions between the management of Pittron Steel Company
and the United Steel Workers Union. Years of "we-they"
thinking had created such tension between union workers
and management that the relationship had exploded into a
bitter eighty-four-day strike. Over the previous three years
the company had posted losses of $6 million. In a manage-
ment shakeup, Wayne was promoted to VP of Operations.
He was concerned about the rampant negative atmosphere
that existed between the managers, the union leaders, and
the workers.

Wayne, a man dedicated to God, sought the advice of
trusted counselors, prayed, and developed an action plan
called Operation Turnaround. He was dedicated to biblical
principles of treating everyone with love, dignity, and respect. If change were to happen, Wayne thought, "It's up to
us. We must take the first step and, if necessary, the second
and third, until things start to change. We're responsible for
what we do, not for what they do in response." His motto
was, "Give—and expect nothing in return."

Wayne began to talk to the men on the production floor.
He held meetings to listen to their ideas and stood at the
gate as they left each night to thank them for their work. He
even started a Bible study in a dingy storage room beneath
the open-hearth furnace. During the gasoline shortage, he
filled the company gas storage tanks and let employees fill
their own cars. Then Wayne did the unthinkable: He
painted his white management hard hat black, the color
worn by the production workers.

Wayne faced criticism, ridicule, and hostility from both sides of the conflict, but he continued to move ahead prayerfully. Over time, progress was made in the face of almost insurmountable odds. A local newspaperman covering this unique story, yelled over to Alderson as he was filling the gas tank of a union worker, "Why are you doing this?" His response was, "Why not?"

Within twenty-one months sales were up 400 percent, profits were up 30 percent, employment had grown by 300 percent, productivity increased by 64 percent, and grievances were reduced from twelve a week to one per year. Soon the company was showing a profit of $6 million—a swing of $12 million.

How can you measure the profit in human terms? A whole plant full of men who had been consumed with anger and bitterness were now coming to work in a spirit of teamwork. Solving the conflict required the right attitude, accessing God, and action. Wayne is now a successful consultant, and I suggest you read this captivating story in R. C. Sproul's book *Stronger Than Steel.*

The Miracle of Pittron, orchestrated by Alderson, should be a ray of hope for all of us. Attitude. Accessing God. Action.

You too will begin to see the glory of God as you look at conflicts in the world of work from a different and exciting perspective. *Blessings to you!*

For Thought and Discussion

1. Do you have a major conflict to resolve in your work life?
2. Is there a step of faith that is needed? What is it?
3. What action is required by you to begin the process?

BIBLIOGRAPHY

Chapter 1
Swindoll, Charles R. *Hand Me Another Brick*, pp. 85–87. Thomas Nelson Publishers, 1978.

Chapter 2
Colson, Chuck, and Jack Eckerd. *Why America Doesn't Work*, pp. xi-xii. Word Publishing, 1991.
Tozer, A. W. *The Pursuit of God*, p. 14. Christian Publications, Inc., 1982.

Chapter 3
Crabb, Larry. *The Marriage Builder*. pp. 70–75. Zondervan Publishing, A Division of HarperCollins, 1992.

Chapter 6
MacAdam, Millard. "A Team Approach to Corporate Mentoring," Vol. 54, No. 1, pp. 9–11. *Contact Quarterly*. The

Magazine for Business by the Christian Businessman's
Committee.

Chapter 11
Wagner, C. Peter. *Your Spiritual Gifts Can Help Your Church Grow*, p. 42. Regal Books, 1979.

Chapter 12
Sproul, R. C. *Stronger Than Steel*. Harper & Row Publishers, 1980.